BUILDING YOUR OWN COMPUTER
MADE EASY

The Step By Step Guide

By James Bernstein

Contents

Introduction

Even though computers have lost some of their popularity thanks to smartphones and tablets, they are still an invaluable tool to have both at home and in the office. There are things you can do with computers that you can't do with your mobile devices and, let's face it, who wants to look at a six inch screen all day?

There are many computer manufacturers that make many different models of computers with various specifications, which gives you a lot of choices but still may not give you everything you want. It's like buying a car that has all the options you want but is missing one feature (such as heated seats) which might make it a deal breaker.

This is where building your own computer comes into play. When you are able to select the exact components you want inside your computer, then you end up with a computer that has everything you want. The only problem is that you can't just go to the store and pick it up and bring it home and plug it in. It will most likely involve several hours of work and a little bit of aggravation along the way.

This book was written to give you a hand in building your new computer by guiding you through the process of selecting the parts, assembling the computer, and then making sure everything works properly after all the pieces are in place. The build process for computers will not be exactly the same for everyone, so keep that in mind when going through this book if something doesn't make sense. You may still need to do a little research on your own for issues related to your specific build.

Once you have everything assembled and get your operating system in place, you can sit back and do all of your customizations and be proud of the monster that you have just created. On that note, let's get building!

Chapter 1 - Why Build Your Own Computer?

Before deciding to build your own computer you may have asked yourself why you wanted to take on the task, or maybe if you really even wanted to at all. Sure it can be intimidating at first (or even after you have built a few), but that doesn't mean it's something you shouldn't try at least once if you are the techy type who likes to have hands-on experience with their electronics.

The Experience
If you plan to maybe work in the computer\IT field or are into electronics as a hobby, then building your own computer is a great way to get some experience with how computers are built and the components that work together to make everything function.

Once you have an understanding of how computers work and what pieces do what, it will help you to troubleshoot and solve computer-related problems that arise. Plus, it will give you the knowledge and confidence to dig into your computer to do things such as replace faulty parts or do upgrades in the future. You will also be a hero to all your friends and family once you start fixing their computer problems.

Many beginning computer classes will require you to have an understanding of how computers work and how to diagnose issues. If you plan on taking a certification test such as the CompTIA A+ exam, then having this experience will definitely be useful to help you pass and get your certification.

Get The Parts You Want
As I just mentioned, when you buy a computer off the shelf you are stuck with the components that it comes with, and it might not be your ideal computer. Sure, you should be able to find something that is close enough, but why settle if you don't have to?

Also keep in mind that even though the computer specs sound good, it doesn't mean they are the greatest quality parts. If a computer at the store boasts 32GB (gigabytes) of RAM (Random Access Memory) that might sound great, but if it's some cheap no-name brand of memory then that might make it not so great. Most computers off the shelf will only give you information about the make and model of the processor and maybe the video card.

Figure 1.1

If you are building a computer for a specific purpose (such as gaming or video editing), then you might need some higher end or more powerful components such as a better video card or a larger amount of RAM. When you choose your own parts then you can get exactly what you need so your new computer will be able to handle whatever you throw at it.

Save Money

Many years ago, building your own computer was a way to save yourself some money since new computers were much more expensive than they are now. So, if you are thinking that building your own computer will be cheaper than buying a new one, this may or may not be the case depending on how you go about it.

If you are just building a computer to be used for the basics such as browsing the Internet and sending emails, then you might be better off just buying something from your local electronics store or online since you can probably get it cheaper than buying all of the parts separately yourself.

But, if you are building a computer with the latest and greatest parts, then it will last you much longer than a cheap one off the shelf because it will stay "up to date" longer than a generic one from the store. I went all out on a computer build and it lasted me over eight years before I replaced it, and was a better performing computer than most of the models you could buy new in the store. The only reason I replaced it was that the power supply went out and I figured why not take the opportunity to start over with something even faster.

When you use quality parts then there is less of a chance of something going out on you requiring that part to be replaced, or even the whole computer needing to be replaced. Certain models also have custom components that might be an odd size to fit in the case, which can limit your options for replacement parts, or you might have to track down an OEM (original equipment manufacturer) part at an increased cost.

So, the bottom line is that building your own computer might not save you money in the short term but should save you money in the long run compared to buying something with no name generic parts from your local electronics store.

Downsides to Building Your Own Computer

Just like with most things, there are downsides to building your own computer, and trying to do so will not be the right choice for everyone. You should really give the process some thought before trying to take on the expensive, time consuming, and even many times frustrating task of building your own computer, especially if you have never done it before and don't have anyone to help you if you get in a jam.

One of the biggest downsides to building your own computer is that you will not have a warranty for the entire thing. Sure you will have a warranty on the parts you use for a limited amount of time, but when something goes wrong, you will be responsible for determining which component is to blame. If you buy a computer off the shelf and it dies then you can simply contact the manufacturer and they will fix it or replace it if it's still in the warranty time period. Depending on where you got the parts to build your computer, it might be harder to get things replaced when they go bad, especially if you got them online.

You might find that you will have a longer warranty on many of your parts than you will have on an entire computer if you were to buy one off the shelf. For example, many processors will have a three year warranty where many computers will have a one year warranty for the entire thing.

Another thing to keep in mind is that if you are having problems with something not working (such as a blank screen when you turn your new computer on), it will be up to you to figure out what the problem might be. (I will be going over some steps to troubleshoot this kind of problem in Chapter 5 just in case it happens to you!)

I mentioned saving money earlier in this chapter, but there is a very good chance that building your own computer will cost you more than you really wanted to spend. Once you start pricing out parts and deciding that you want the "good stuff", then the total cost of your build can start to skyrocket. But if money is not an object and you want the best you can get, then I suppose there is nothing to worry about.

One other downside to building your own computer I want to mention is that when your operating system decides to call it quits and gets to a point where you can't get your computer running again, then you will be looking at starting from scratch.

Most new computers come with a recovery partition or recovery disk that lets you restore the computer back to the way it was when you bought it with all the drivers and any software that came with it intact. If you install your own OS and can't get your computer going again, then you will be forced to start from scratch. One way around this is to get your computer to the way you want it and then make an image of the entire OS and programs that can be restored in case something goes wrong. Keep in mind that if you do have to restore your image, it will only bring you as current as the date it was created on. Many operating systems (such as Windows) have built-in recovery features that will allow you to do this.

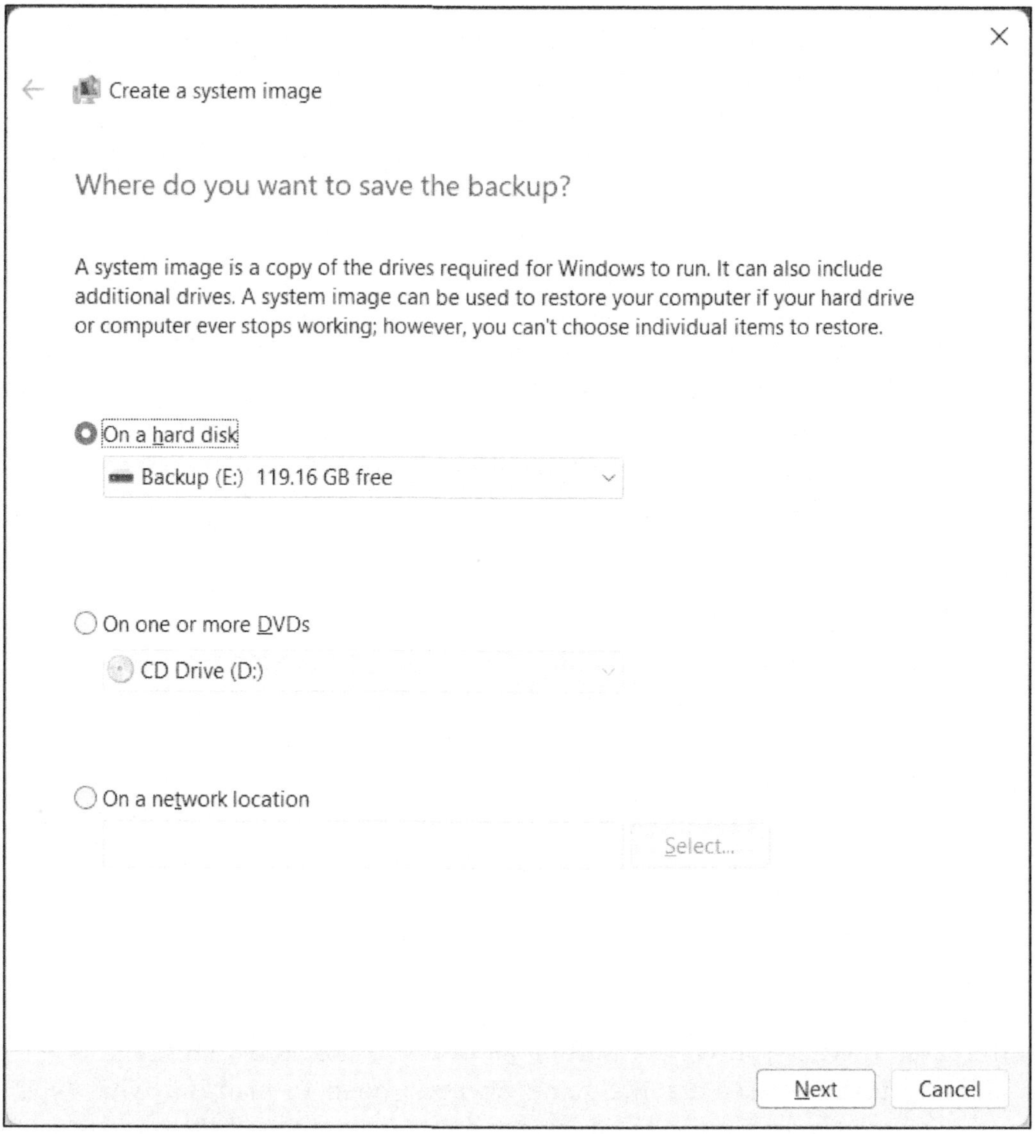

Figure 1.2

As you can see, building your own computer has its pros and cons, so before deciding to take on the challenge, you should make sure you are up to it and come up with a game plan so the process will go as smoothly as possible. I will say that once you build your first computer it's way easier the second time, and even more so the time after that.

Chapter 2 - Choosing Components

As I mentioned in the last chapter, being able to choose the components you want for your computer rather than assuming they are something decent when you buy one already built is one of the benefits of building your own computer. But if this is your first build, and you are not familiar with what components are better than the next and are not sure what you want, then there will be some research involved on your end.

The first thing you need to do when choosing components is to figure out what you will be doing with your new computer, and which of these things will require the most "horsepower" to run smoothly. For example, if you are intending to play video games with detailed graphics, you will want to get a higher end video card that can handle it, otherwise you might be dealing with performance issues or having to turn the graphics quality down to have the gameplay smoothly.

The Parts You Will Need
All computers will pretty much contain the same components, but there are some that are optional, such as a floppy disk drive (kidding!). As I mentioned before, what you plan on doing with the computer will determine what parts go into the computer, so you should make a list, decide what you want, and put a price next to it so you can add everything up and see what kind of cost you will be looking at.

Here is a rundown of the parts you will need and a brief description of what they each do:

Case
The case is what you will be putting all of the components into, and don't go thinking that all cases are the same. You will need to plan out what type of motherboard you are going to be using and get a case that will allow you to mount that particular type of motherboard. For example, there are ATX desktops, ATX full tower, ATX mid-tower, ATX mini-tower, mini ITX cases, and so on. (ATX stands for *Advanced Technology eXtended,* in case you were wondering.) There are other types as well, but for the typical home user, you will be sticking with one of the ATX classes of cases.

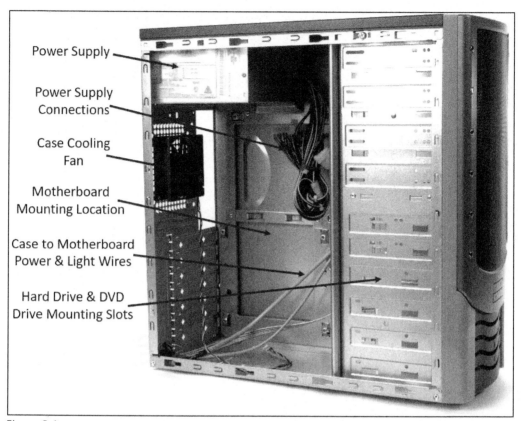

Power Supply

Power Supply Connections

Case Cooling Fan

Motherboard Mounting Location

Case to Motherboard Power & Light Wires

Hard Drive & DVD Drive Mounting Slots

Figure 2.1

Other things you need to look for in a case is if it will have the room to house all of your components that are not being installed on the motherboard, such as your hard drive(s) and DVD drives. There is nothing worse than getting your motherboard installed and then realizing you don't have enough room for a particular component and having to figure out a workaround.

Also, make sure the power supply mounting location will not affect mounting the motherboard or make it difficult to install your hard drives etc. Some cases will come with a power supply already installed, and if you plan on adding additional fans to the case, make sure there is a place to mount those as well. Most cases will also come with a fan or fans installed, but many people like to add additional fans to increase the airflow inside the case. Speaking of airflow, make sure the case has adequate ventilation as well.

Your case buttons and lights will connect to the motherboard via wires in order to do things like turn the power on and show hard drive activity and the power light etc. Most of the time the connections will all work okay, but you might want to make sure that all the case wires have a place to go on the motherboard. (I will

11

discuss how these wires connect when I discuss assembling the components inside the case.)

Most cases will come with multiple hard drives and DVD drive bays. For the most part, your DVD drive will be put in a 5.25 inch slot. Hard drives will take a 3.5 inch slot or go in a 5.25 inch slot with an adapter. SSD (solid state) hard drives tend to be smaller and will go in a 2.5 inch slot or a larger slot with an adapter. Always make sure that you have enough of the right type of slots (or adapters) to hold the drives that you will be installing.

You can tell a cheap case from a quality case by the way it is built and the materials used in its construction. Getting a nicer case will make installing your parts easier and give you an overall better build. Things will also tend to fit better in a nicely built case. A nice case will cost you around $75 or more, and some of them can be over $200! If you plan on using your own power supply, then you can save some money and get one without the power supply installed.

 I prefer larger cases since they give you more options as to where you can install your components and they also leave room for expansion. Plus, if you plan on working on your computer in the future, you will be glad you have the extra room when you need to get your hands in there!

Power Supply
The power supply is what gives the computer and all of its components the power to operate. These power supplies are installed inside of the case and will have a variety of wired connections with different types of connectors for things like hard drives, DVD drives, high end video cards, motherboard power, and so on.

Figure 2.2

It's important to get the right types of connections on your power supply to fit your motherboard and other components. A few years back you had to worry about IDE and SATA hard drive and DVD drive power connections, so you had to choose your power supply based on what types of drives you had. For the most part, you won't be using any old school IDE drives unless you happen to have one laying around you plan on using. If that's the case, then there are IDE to SATA conversion adapters you can use. Figure 2.3 shows some of the various types of power connectors you will see with today's power supplies.

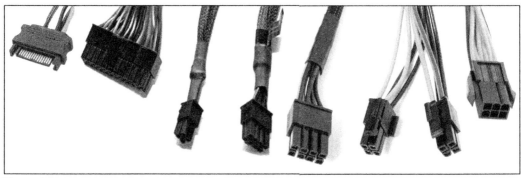

Figure 2.3

Higher end power supplies will have removable cables so you can attach only the types you need and not have a lot of extra power connections that are not being used sitting around inside your case and getting in the way. Cheaper power supplies will have the cables hard wired to the power supply, and you pretty much get what they give you and hope that you have enough of the connection types you need.

Some motherboards will have a four pin CPU power connector, and some will have an eight pin connector. It's a good idea to get a power supply with a 4+4 connector, which will allow you to use either one since there will be two 4 pin connectors, which will allow you to use one or both of them.

Figure 2.4

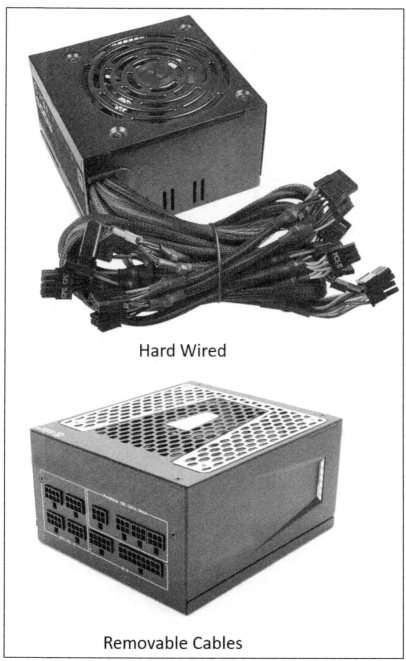

Hard Wired

Removable Cables

Figure 2.5

ATX power supplies use a single 20-pin connector as the main power connector and a 4-pin +12V connector to deliver power specifically to the processor (as shown in figure 2.5). I have seen people (including myself) forget to plug in the 4 pin connector and wonder why their computer won't power up, so be sure to make a note of this!

Figure 2.6

Deciding how much power your power supply needs to put out is another factor that you will need to determine based on your hardware. If you plan on having a high end video card and multiple hard drives and fans, then you will need a power supply that can handle the load. It's always better to go overboard compared to not getting one powerful enough.

Fortunately, there are websites that can help you determine the correct output needed for your power supply. Back in the old days you just had to guess or do a bunch of math to try and figure it out. PC power supply ratings are based on wattage, so that's what most people go by when choosing how "large" of a power supply to use for their computer. Some computers with basic hardware can have a power supply that is only rated at 200W, while higher end computers such as gaming computers can have a power supply closer to 1000W (and even higher). A gaming video card can require 200W of power just for itself. Of course, the higher wattage power supplies will cost more money, so once you determine what hardware is going into your computer, look online for a power supply calculator to get an idea of how powerful of a power supply you will need.

Motherboard
Think of the motherboard as the brain of the computer because it ties into and controls all of the other components (or organs, if you will) and allows all of the

parts to communicate with each other. As I mentioned in my discussion of cases, there are various motherboard size specifications, so, once again, make sure to match up your motherboard with your case.

The motherboard will have various slots and sockets that you will connect things like your processor, RAM, and video card to. It's important to get a motherboard that will work with the type of processor and RAM you will be using. For example, there are Intel and AMD processors and a wide variety of models from each one, so if your motherboard doesn't support the one you are using, then you will be going nowhere fast. There are also different types of RAM running at different speeds, so you should check that out as well to make sure your motherboard will support the RAM you intend to use.

Figure 2.7

Also, be sure to check the expansion slot and port types to be sure it has enough of the type you need. There will be RAM slots, PCIe (express) slots, SATA ports, fan power ports, and so on. A while back there used to be many additional types of ports such as AGP and ISA slots, but now, for the most part, your components will use a PCIe slot.

There are generally two types of PCIe slots in use today: x16 and x1 (even though there are x2, x4 and x8 slots out there, too). These numbers refer to the bandwidth capabilities of the slots. As a rule of thumb, your video card should go into the first PCI Express x16 slot. That doesn't mean it won't work if you put it in a different one, but it might run a little slower based on your motherboard configuration. The slots are usually numbered on the motherboard starting with either a 0 or a 1. If you plan on making a serious gaming computer, keep in mind that some of the gaming video cards are huge, and will block off the slot next to the one it uses, taking away one of your available slots.

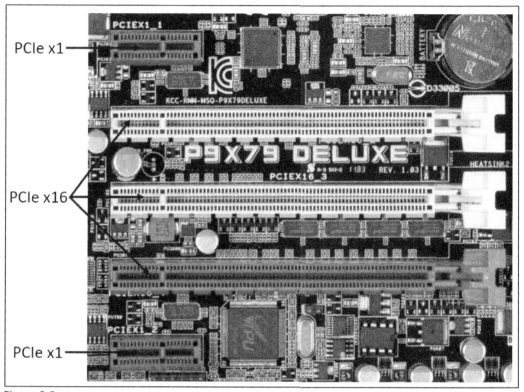

Figure 2.8

Another thing you will need to take into account is how many drives you will be installing in your computer. By drives I mean hard drives (SSD and SATA) or DVD drives. The motherboard will have SATA (Serial ATA) ports on it that are used to connect these types of drives, so make sure you have enough for your build.

You should have at least four SATA ports on your motherboard (or possibly more), and you might notice that they are not all the same color (as in figure 2.9). They will most likely be a combination of black, blue, or red.

Figure 2.9

This is usually because the ports are used for different types of connections and they may be one of the following:

- Primary SATA controller ports
- Secondary SATA controller ports
- RAID capable SATA controller ports

You will need to check your motherboard manual to see what ports are used for what functionality since the color schemes aren't universal between motherboard manufacturers.

Always check the upgrade capabilities of the motherboard before you buy it. Make sure it has enough RAM slots if you want to expand later and find out the maximum amount of RAM it can use. Also be sure that it has enough expansion slots for any cards you might add in the future.

I'm sure you have noticed all of the connections on the back of your computer but might not have realized that most of them are integrated into the motherboard. This makes things simple because everything you need can be included with the motherboard. On the other hand, if one or more of these connections\ports goes bad, then it's not something you can replace without maybe adding a secondary card with more of those connections on it. For example, if the onboard video port goes out, then you will be forced to get a standalone video card that you will have to install in the computer to get your video output back.

Figure 2.10 shows many of the typical connections\ports that you will find included with a motherboard. This doesn't mean they are all the same and some might have different types of connections or more of a certain type of port etc.

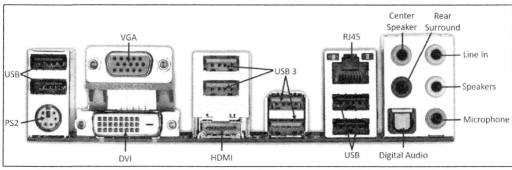

Figure 2.10

Here is a listing of the most common connections and ports you will find built into a motherboard.

- **USB** – Universal Serial Bus ports are the current king of connectivity for devices that you connect to your computer (such as printers, keyboards, mice, smartphones, and so on). Currently, there are three standards of USB ports, which include 1.x, 2.0, and the current 3.x. As USB technology progressed, the data transfer speeds kept increasing. You won't see any USB 1.x ports on current motherboards, but you will still see 2.0 ports (for now) and 3.x ports, which are usually colored blue or red and often labeled SS for SuperSpeed. The newer ports are backward compatible with older USB devices so you can use any port you want for any device.

- **PS2** – It's rare if you will still see any PS2 ports on newer computers. These were generally used for connecting mice and keyboards to the computer—which had PS2 connections on them. So, if you see one on a new motherboard, it's most likely for backward compatibility.

- **VGA** – Video Graphics Array connections are used to connect a monitor to a computer to transfer video signals from the computer back to the monitor. VGA ports are starting to get phased out for more advanced connection types that offer a digital connection rather than an analog one.

- **DVI** – Digital Visual Interface connections are also used to connect a monitor to a computer to transfer video signals, but in the case of DVI they use a digital signal rather than an analog signal. There is a standard called DVI-A that is actually analog, but you won't be using that type. Even DVI connections are starting to be phased out for newer technology such as HDMI and DisplayPort.

- **HDMI** – High Definition Multimedia Interface is another type of video connection that you might be familiar with because it's commonly used with TVs to connect to cable boxes and DVD\Blu Ray players. Many newer monitors will use an HDMI port to connect it to the computer.

- **DisplayPort** – This is yet another video connection type that can also carry audio, USB, and other forms of data (figure 2.11). It's not as common as the other video connection types, but you still might see it integrated with your motherboard. You will need a DisplayPort connection on your monitor to use it, though.

Figure 2.11

- **RJ45** – An RJ45 port is used for connecting a network cable, allowing your computer to communicate with other computers and devices on a network. It's also used to connect to your broadband modem for your Internet connection. If you don't plan on connecting to the Internet wirelessly, then you will need to use the RJ45 port to do so.

- **Digital\Optical Audio** – This port uses fiber optic audio cables and laser light to transmit digital audio signals between devices such as your computer and sound system. It's not very common these days since HDMI can carry audio signals as well as your video signal.

- **Sound Card Ports** – Motherboards come with integrated sound cards that offer most of the functionality of a standalone sound card (unless you get into the higher level sound cards). There will be various ports for things such as your speakers, a microphone, headphones, and other outputs.

Choosing a motherboard will require some research on your end and reading reviews from reputable websites and forums always helps. Just like with anything, some brands are better than others, but at the same time one brand can make a great motherboard model and still make a bad one as well.

Processor\CPU & Heatsink

If the motherboard is the brain of the computer, then the processor would be the heart since it powers the whole operation (not like the way a power supply does, but in terms of processing power). Processors are also referred to as CPUs (Central Processing Unit), so if you hear it both ways, just know it's referring to the same thing.

There are many processors to choose from, providing different levels of performance and, of course, price points. For the most part, you will be choosing between a processor made by Intel or by AMD (Advanced Micro Devices). Generally, Intel processors are more expensive and are used for higher end applications such as the servers in your data center at work. However, this doesn't mean that AMD processors are no good, and your choice should be based on what you plan to do with your computer and your budget. Plus many people prefer AMD processors for gaming computers.

Figure 2.12

Clock Speeds

Processor performance is measured at a speed called clock speed. This is measured in Gigahertz (or GHz). It is the speed at which a microprocessor executes instructions. Back in the day of single core processors, you could easily compare performance by clock speed, but with today's multi core processors (discussed next), things are a little more complicated. Plus, the clock speed of one model of processor compared to another model is not necessarily an exact measurement of how fast they are in relation to each other.

Normally you will see CPU speed displayed in numbers, such as 3.7GHz and so on. This is a good starting point to know what type of performance you will be getting, but there are other factors to consider. Plus modern processors can vary their speeds based on how much load is placed on them. Some of these processors can be what they call "overclocked", which increases the clock rate of the processor. It can also make it run hot or malfunction if overdone or done incorrectly.

Once you decide on what manufacturer and family of processor you want to use, then you can read up on the specs for each processor and compare all their differences. Just keep in mind that the clock speed is not the only thing you should be looking at.

 Be aware that there are various versions (or generations, as they are called) of processors. For example, Intel has been making their i7 processor for over ten years, so be sure you are getting a current generation. If the price is too good to be true, then it might be an older one.

Processor Cores

If you have been checking out processors, you will most likely have read about references to the number of cores a processor has. Originally processors only had one core, which had to do all of the work. A core is a processing unit that reads instructions to perform specific actions or tasks. So, when you have more than one core, the computer can run different actions on different cores at the same time rather than having to wait for the single core to be free.

Think of cores as processors within a processor. If you have a four core processor, there are technically four processors within that one chip. There are also physical cores and virtual\logical cores. A logical core is a physical core that is logically split up into multiple virtual cores. Think of a virtual core as how many threads the physical core can process at the same time whereas a thread is a sequence of instructions.

You generally don't need a bunch of cores within your processor since many programs won't make use of all of them unless you are running processor-intensive applications such as video editing or modeling apps. Today's CPUs are now offering huge numbers such as eighteen cores on one processor, which is overkill for most users. Usually something like a four or eight core processor will do the trick for running your typical applications.

Hyper-threading

Hyper-threading is a technique that has been around for years and is used to get more performance out of a CPU core. By using hyper-threading, you can make one physical processor appear as two logical processors. This is not as effective as having actual additional cores, but hyper-threading aware applications can still benefit from it.

Hyper-threading is used only on Intel chips and is their version of simultaneous multithreading (SMT), which is what AMD calls their version. So, if you have a four core processor with hyper-threading technology, it will act like an eight core processor. This allows the two logical processor cores to share physical execution resources. This can increase performance because if one logical CPU is stalled and waiting, the other logical CPU can borrow its execution resources. However, your operating system and BIOS\motherboard must support hyper-threading in order to use the feature.

Cache

Processors have a built-in hardware cache to help reduce waiting time for accessing data from the processor's main memory and also RAM. This cache is a faster type of memory, and data in this cache is information that is more frequently used. By keeping it in the cache, it can be accessed more quickly. The processor will check its cache for the data it needs before going to RAM since the CPU cache is much faster (and more expensive) than RAM.

Processors will have multiple levels of cache memory which are usually labeled L1, L2, and L3, with L1 cache being the fastest (and usually the smallest). L2 is a secondary larger cache that may or may not be on a separate chip. L3 cache is designed to improve the performance of the L1 and L2 cache. Don't focus too much on cache sizes when it comes to selecting a processor because it's not as much of a factor when it comes to performance as it used to be.

RAM (Random Access Memory)

RAM is used as the computer's main memory to store running programs that are being used by the computer. Since RAM is a fast type of memory, the computer can access this data as quickly as needed when that data is stored in its RAM. Don't get RAM numbers confused with hard drive storage numbers because they are *not* the same thing. You might have 16GB (gigabytes) of RAM and 1000GB of storage memory, but they are completely different things.

Figure 2.13

Today's computers use DRAM (Dynamic Random Access Memory), or, more specifically, synchronous DRAM (or SDRAM). You will usually see the acronym DDR being used when shopping for RAM, which stands for double data rate and refers to how much data the memory can transfer in one clock cycle. Currently, DDR5 is the latest and greatest version of this memory.

RAM comes in various size DIMMS (or sticks, as they are often called), and you can only have as much RAM as you have RAM slots for on your motherboard. Most motherboards will come with at least four slots. So, if you want 16GB of RAM in your computer, you can get one 16GB stick, two 8GB sticks, or four 4GB sticks, depending on what works best for your budget. Just keep in mind that if you use all of your RAM slots with smaller sticks, then if you want to upgrade you will not be able to add more sticks, but instead will have to replace the ones you have with larger ones. I recommend starting out with a minimum of 8GB of RAM. If you are building a gaming computer, then go for at least 16GB or maybe even 32GB.

Many motherboards have dual channel slots, so it's a good idea to install your RAM in pairs on the motherboard. The slots will usually be color coded to tell you which pair go together. Be sure to use identical speed RAM when pairing your memory. (Things will still work fine if you use one chip rather than two.)

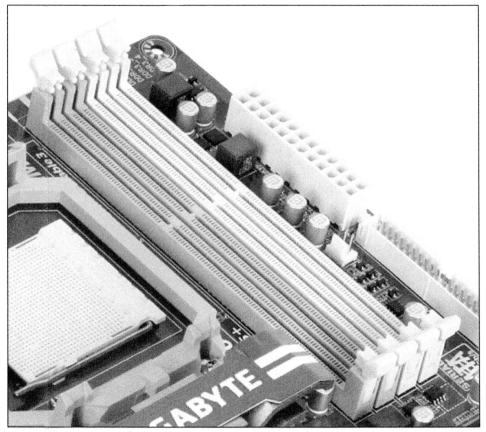

Figure 2.14

RAM speed (its data transfer rate) is measured in megahertz (MHz), or millions of cycles per second (which is a similar measurement to your processor's clock speed which is measured in gigahertz (GHz), which is *billions* of cycles per second). You might see speeds shown as 2133MHz, and you might also see it displayed like PC4-28800 or DDR4 3600, which can make things a little confusing when shopping for

RAM. The bottom line is that faster is always better, but having more RAM will help you out more than having faster RAM. Just remember to make sure you get RAM that works with your motherboard because it's not all plug and play. Also, try to match the speed of each of your RAM sticks, otherwise it will run at the speed of the slowest one.

The speed of your processor and the bus speed of the system motherboard both play a part when it comes to the speed of RAM installed in your system. If all the parts that need to talk to each other can't communicate at the same speed, then the slowest component will determine the overall speed of the system. This is often referred to as a bottleneck.

Hard Drive

As I am sure you know, when you use a computer you will need a place to store files and install programs, so that is where the hard drive comes into play. The hard drive is a device that is installed inside the computer and is attached to the motherboard, then accessed by the system to open files and run programs. These hard drives come in more than one type and have a variety of storage capabilities.

You will find that you can get either an SSD (solid state disk) hard drive or a SATA (serial attached SCSI) hard drive for your computer. There are other types such as SAS and SCSI hard drives, but those are used mostly in datacenters for servers etc. SSD drives will be more expensive than SATA drives, so the choice is up to you and your budget as to which type you want to use.

SSD Hard Drive

SATA Hard Drive

Figure 2.15

SSD drives use flash memory for storage (like a USB drive) and don't have any moving parts, making them much faster than other drives. Therefore, data transfer rates for SSD drives are faster than other types. They also use less power than drives with moving parts. The information on SSD drives is stored in microchips and has its own processor to perform the operations related to reading and writing data.

As of this writing, the storage capacities of SSD drives are not as large as that of SATA drives (unless you want to mortgage your house to get one), but they keep increasing as technology improves. The price per terabyte of SSD drives is much higher than that of SATA drives.

SATA drives use a high speed serial cable to attach to the motherboard and are much faster than the older IDE hard drives that are now pretty much obsolete. SATA drives do have moving parts (like the older IDE drives) which consist of several platters that store the data and a moving head that reads and writes data to and from these platters.

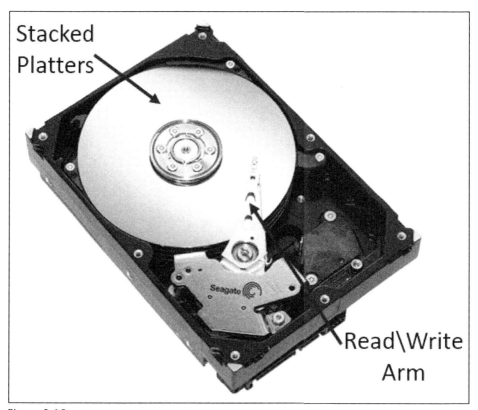

Figure 2.16

Both of these types of hard drives use SATA connectors to connect to the motherboard, so your motherboard will be able to use either type of drive. SATA drives are usually 3.5" in size, but they can also come in the smaller 2.5" size. SSD drives are usually 2.5" in size, but you can find some that are 3.5".

 If you want to see fast boot up times then go for an SSD drive for your operating system. On my computer it only takes five seconds from when I press the power button to when I see the Windows login screen, which is way faster than things used to be!

As for capacity, you need to determine what kinds of files you will be storing and how large your programs will be. What I like to do is use an SSD drive to install Windows and my programs on, and then have a separate and larger SATA drive to keep my files on. This way if Windows (or another operating system) crashes, all of your files will not be affected. Plus, having the operating system and programs on a faster drive improves their performance and startup speed. I would get at least a 512GB SSD drive for the OS and programs and a 2TB drive for your files. If you can afford to go bigger, then you should, since you most likely will need it in the future.

DVD Drive

If you plan on installing software from CDs or DVDs and also plan on watching movies or making music CDs, then you will need a DVD drive. Many computers are being shipped without DVD drives, but I still feel they are not ready to be obsolete just quite yet.

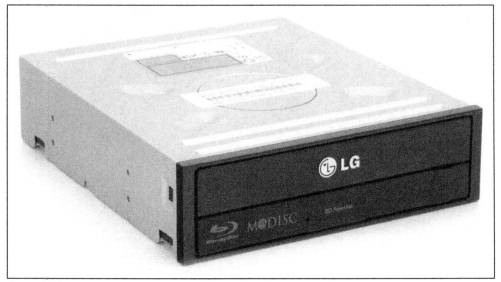

Figure 2.17

Nowadays people download their music and software from the Internet, but there will still be times when having a DVD drive will come in handy. If you want to burn music CDs, make a wedding video DVD, or just watch a movie, then having a DVD drive is important. Plus, they are very cheap (at around $40 or so), and these DVD drives will also support playing and writing to regular CDs.

Installing a DVD drive will take up one of your SATA ports on the motherboard, so keep that in mind if you are planning on having multiple hard drives. For most people there will be enough SATA ports to be able to use one for your DVD drive. You can also get an external CD\DVD drive that connects via USB.

Video Card (optional)

As I mentioned earlier, your motherboard will have a built-in video card allowing you to send video signals from your computer to the monitor. The only problem with using the onboard video is that it's really only meant to be used for general purpose tasks like working on spreadsheets and checking email (etc.).

If you plan on playing graphic intensive video games or editing high resolution videos, then you might want to think about getting a standalone video card that you will insert into one of your PCIe slots on the motherboard.

Figure 2.18

These high-end video cards have their own processors and memory dedicated to video performance, and oftentimes have their own fans to keep all that horsepower cool. Plus, most of the time they will need their own dedicated power connection from the power supply, which means you need a power supply that can handle the extra load.

Sound Card (optional)

Another optional component you can add to your computer is a sound card. The sound card transfers the sounds from your computer to your speakers. All motherboards should have a built-in sound card with various audio ports, but there are some people who like to go all out and get a higher end standalone sound card to optimize their audio experience.

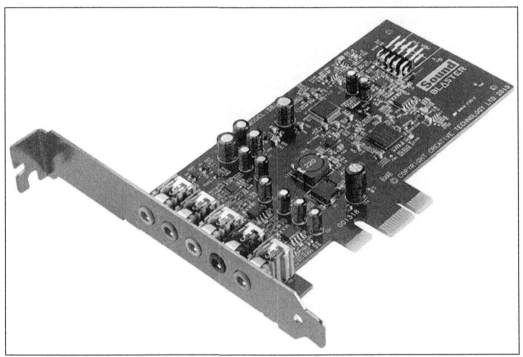

Figure 2.19

Speakers will make more of a difference in audio quality than the sound card, so if you have a top of the line sound card and low quality speakers, then you are just wasting your money. Many onboard soundcards won't offer as many channels as standalone cards, so if you have a 7.1 surround sound speaker system and your onboard soundcard doesn't support 7.1, then that would be a reason for an upgrade. I have never had an onboard soundcard that doesn't do a good enough job when it comes to playing movies and music, but then again I have some nice speakers, which make all the difference.

If you need a specific connection type in addition to the standard ports on a typical sound card, then you might be forced into getting a standalone sound card.

Figure 2.20

Network Card (optional)

Connecting to the Internet is one of the main reasons that people get a computer, and having a fast connection is a top priority for most people who spend a lot of time online. In this case, it's a must to have a fast network connection since when you connect to the Internet you are connecting to the largest network of them all.

There are two main ways that people connect to the Internet and also to networks, and they are through their RJ45 network port (figure 2.21) or via a wireless connection. Back in the earlier days of computers, you would have to install a standalone network card if you wanted to get on the Internet, and Wi-Fi wasn't even really a thing yet.

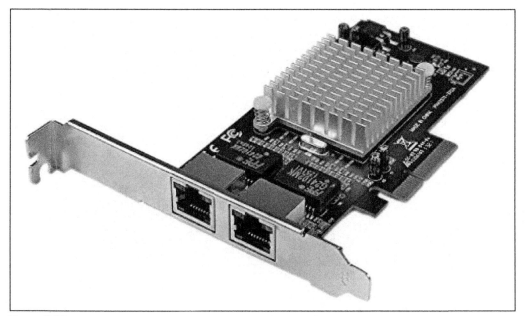

Figure 2.21

All modern motherboards will have a network port built in, even though I can actually see them being phased out to some degree (for home computers) since electronics manufacturers are making everything wireless these days. These network ports have various speed capabilities which determines how fast they can transfer data over a network or the Internet.

All modern network cards should support a data transfer rate of at least 1 Gbps (gigabyte per second), so if you see anything slower like 10/100 Mbps (megabyte per second), you will know it's an outdated model.

All you should need is one of these network ports on your computer, and the only reason to have additional ports is if you were doing some type of dual-homed server configuration where you need to connect to two different networks at the same time.

Wireless Adapter (optional)
As I just mentioned before, everything seems to be wireless these days, and now desktop computer manufacturers are making built-in wireless capabilities standard practice now. Just a few years ago, built-in wireless was only standard on laptop computers.

When you build your own computer you may or may not choose one with built-in Wi-Fi capabilities, and even if you do then it might not be up to the performance that you desire. This is where adding a standalone wireless adapter can help you out.

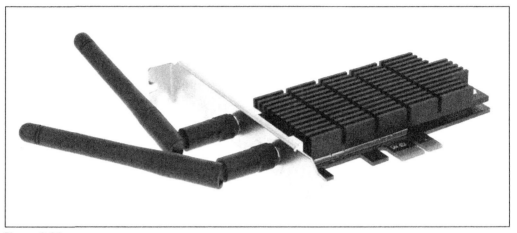

Figure 2.22

I have noticed that desktop computers with built-in wireless can suffer a little when it comes to signal strength, and that might be because the wireless adapter is on the motherboard and therefore inside the case, so you might want to try the built in Wi-Fi before spending the money on a wireless card.

An easier way to go is to just use an external USB wireless adapter rather than having to plug a card into your motherboard. These can connect to any USB port, and then you simply install a driver for them and configure your network\Internet access.

One thing to keep in mind for wireless cards is line of sight to your wireless router. If you have your computer under a desk with the antenna sticking out the back, it might not get as good of a signal compared to having a USB adapter with a cable that allows you to put in on your desk.

Figure 2.23

There is not a whole lot of difference between using a wireless card vs. a wireless USB adapter (assuming they are of the same quality). Many wireless cards (and some USB adapters) have detachable antennas so you can install a larger or more powerful one if needed. You will usually have more antenna options with the standalone card than you will with the USB adapter, as well as the ability to use multiple antennas.

One thing to remember is that using a wireless card will take up a PCI slot on your motherboard, which you might or might not be able to spare. On the other hand, a USB wireless adapter will take up a USB port on your computer, which you might or might not be able to spare.

What You Should Look for
When shopping for parts, reviews are your friends, and so are name brand components. And when I say reviews I just don't mean Amazon customer reviews, but rather when real computer sites do reviews and actual testing of a product.

Once you start looking around enough, you will start to become familiar with which companies are known for making which components. You will also see the same companies making different parts, but that doesn't mean they are good at everything. It's like buying a car from the same manufacturer that makes your refrigerator. Sure, they might make a great refrigerator, but that doesn't mean they make good cars, too.

When you see a part that is super cheap, there is usually a reason for it. If you want your computer to last and to perform well, you should be prepared to spend the money to do it right. If you don't mind last year's components, you can usually get the models that they are phasing out at a discount and it will still be quality stuff.

Be sure to always look at all the specifications so that all of your components will be guaranteed to work together properly. Many websites will allow you to do a side by side comparison of two or more brands or models to see how they stack up to each other feature wise.

You might want to take the time and do something like a spreadsheet and create different combinations of parts to see how they will add up price wise so you can see how good of a computer you can afford to build. Then you can mix and match parts to get the best components you can get while staying within your budget.

Where to get your parts
With online shopping the way it is now, you might be tempted to buy everything online, which can be a good way to save money. But, at the same time, it makes things more difficult when it comes to returns and exchanges. It's fairly common to have to exchange a part or two when building a computer, mostly when something doesn't work properly. The most commonly exchanged parts (in my experience) are motherboards and RAM. It's very frustrating turning on your newly built computer and having a black screen or not even getting it to power up at all!

There are many online retailers that sell computer parts such as Amazon, NewEgg, TigerDirect, Best Buy, and even eBay. Some of these retailers even have actual stores, such as Best Buy, so if you need to do a return or exchange, you can do so at the store rather than having to ship it back. Just keep in mind that they might not have the same part to exchange in stock.

I prefer to buy some of the more sensitive parts—like the motherboard, RAM, and processor—locally in case I have an issue and need to return it. Plus, you can talk to people in the store if you have any questions on any components or need any advice. Some stores have more informed employees than others, though.

I have also seen prepackaged bundles where the parts have been selected for you and you can get a parts package based on what type of computer you are trying to build. When you do it this way, you are guaranteed that all of the parts will work with each other.

Chapter 3 – Planning Your Build

Now that you have all of your components selected and hopefully in your possession and not in a box on a truck somewhere, it's time to start planning your build. It's not a good idea to just start throwing parts together without a game plan, so having one helps to make sure you do things right and don't forget anything important that might be hard to figure out later on.

As I mentioned before, after you build your first computer things will be much easier the next time around, and if you do it enough times you can do it blindfolded (not really). I know it can be intimidating when you have a bunch of expensive parts lying on a table and you're afraid of handling something the wrong way (or, even worse, *breaking* something), but as long as you are careful and follow some basic guidelines, everything should work out just fine—assuming you don't have any faulty components!

Getting Organized
The first thing you want to do is get yourself organized and make sure you are really ready to start your build. First of all, you should make sure that you are not missing any parts, and by that I mean open up all of your boxes and make sure nothing was forgotten. For example, make sure your processor came with a heatsink and fan etc. I didn't mention heatsinks in the last chapter, but if you don't know what is, then take a look at figure 3.1.

Figure 3.1

The fan mounts on top of the heatsink, and then the whole unit is mounted on top of the processor on the motherboard. The heatsink is designed to dissipate heat from the processor and keep it cool. Without a heatsink and fan, your processor would overheat and die within minutes.

Other things to look for include any cables that you might need such as SATA cables (figure 3.2) to connect your hard drive and DVD drive as well as having enough and the right type of power cables coming off of your power supply for all of your components. You can get these cables with straight ends or 45 degree angled ends for those hard to reach places.

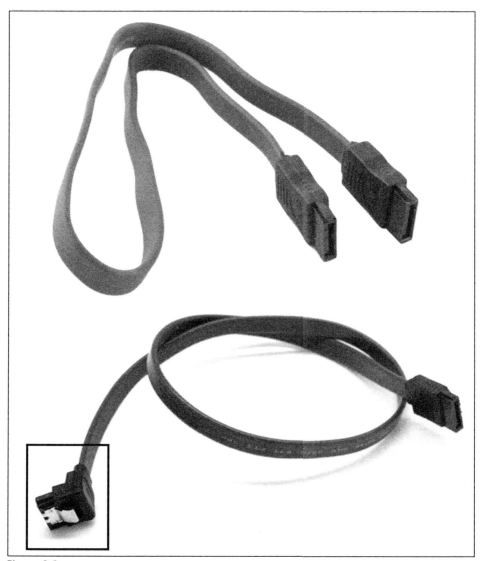

Figure 3.2

Your motherboard and\or case should come with motherboard standoffs (figure 3.2) and screws that are used to mount your motherboard to the case. The standoffs are screwed into the case, and then the motherboard is screwed into the top of the standoffs so the board and circuitry doesn't physically touch the case.

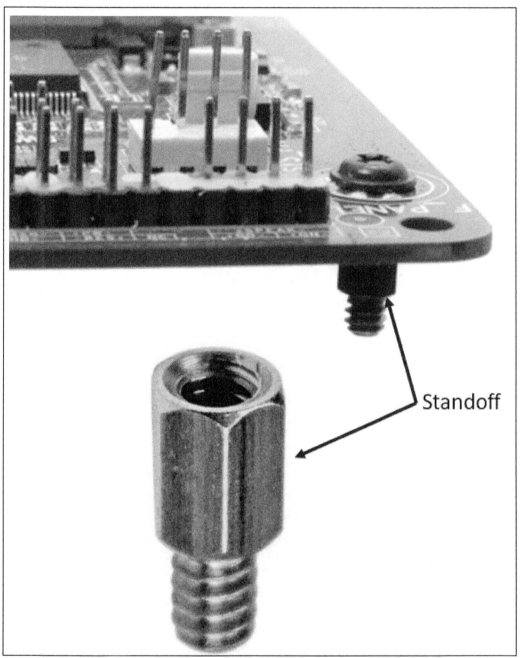

Standoff

Figure 3.3

Also, be sure that your hard drive and DVD drive have screws with them since they are a specific size made to fit with the drive. If you are using a drive adapter to make the drive fit into the case, then be sure those are either included with the case, or you got some separately. Also make sure they are the right size and that everything lines up.

Figure 3.4

If you decided to go with any standalone cards (such as a video or sound card), make sure you got the right type that will work with your motherboard expansion slots and that they will fit on the motherboard and in the case without getting in the way or anything. Some of those video cards can be huge and might block off things like RAM access etc.

One thing that is very important to figure out is *where* you are going to assemble your computer. You should find a table with lots of extra room so you can spread things out without having to stack parts boxes on top of each other. This will give you a nice overview of what you have and what needs to be done.

Find a couple of bowls or Tupperware containers for screws so you don't have to put them on the table and risk having them roll off onto the floor. Try not to mix up screws from different parts if you can, otherwise you will be doing some trial and error trying to find the right screw for the right component.

Required Tools
In order to build a computer, you don't need sophisticated tools. Just some basic hand tools will do. There are five basic tools you will need to get the job done, and having some extra types of tools laying around might come in handy.

- Flathead Screwdriver
- Phillips Head Screwdriver
- Needle Nose Pliers
- ¼ Inch Nut Driver
- Zip Ties

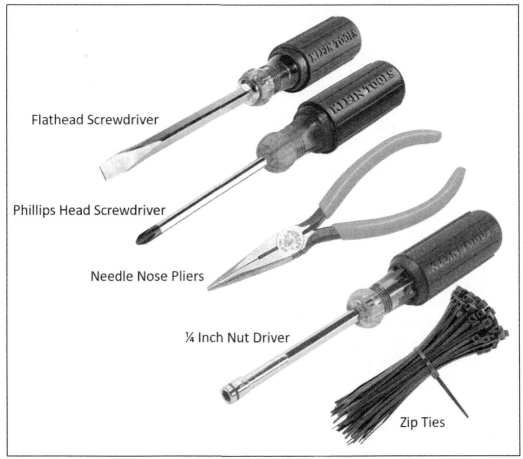

Flathead Screwdriver

Phillips Head Screwdriver

Needle Nose Pliers

¼ Inch Nut Driver

Zip Ties

Figure 3.5

You might be able to get away with not using the nut driver, but it can be easier to use when tightening screws than using a screwdriver since many of the screws will let you use either tool on them.

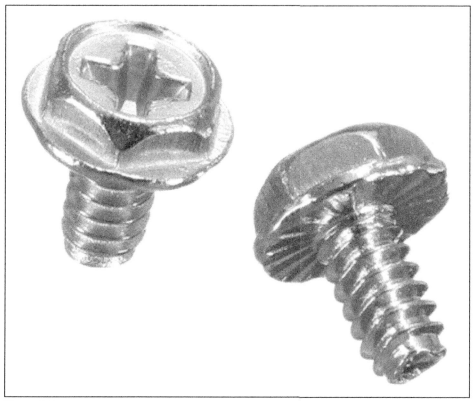

Figure 3.6

Zip ties are used to wrap up cables to get them out of the way of other parts and fans and also to make the inside of the case look cleaner and more organized. Just be sure not to make them super tight, or you might run into some trouble trying to cut them off without damaging a wire if you need to remove them.

One other tool you might want to get is an anti-static wrist strap to avoid any issues with static electricity damaging your new components. You don't want to transfer any jolts of electricity through your expensive parts by shocking them with your hands.

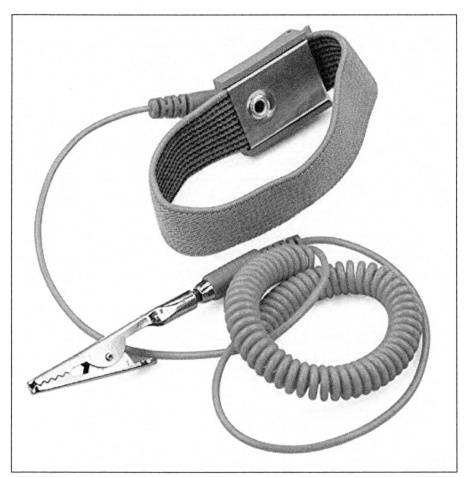

Figure 3.7

As you can see in figure 3.7, there is a strap that you wrap around your wrist with the metal part touching your skin. This strap is then connected to a cord with an alligator clip on the end. You connect the alligator clip to something that is unpainted metal on your case. (Many people like to attach it to a screw on the power supply.) Before attaching it, make sure to turn your power supply off and plug the power cord into the outlet. There will be a power on and off switch on the back of the power supply.

I personally don't use anti-static wrist straps but make sure to touch something metal that is not related to the computer or the parts before touching anything to discharge any static electricity. You might want to avoid standing on carpet when building your computer and not do it on windy days where there is a higher chance of static electricity.

Getting Help If Needed

Before starting your build, you might want to see if you can have a friend with computer building experience on hand if you run into any problems. Or, better yet, have your friend there to help you out!

Another good idea is to get yourself familiar with computer related forums online and maybe sign up for a couple of them. That way if you have a question, you can post it on the forum and see if you can get a helpful response. The only problem with this is sometimes you will have to wait a while before somebody responds and then the advice they give you might not be what you are looking for.

If you have a local computer shop in your area you can always take your computer there and have them try and figure out the problem for you. They may give you some free advice or they may want to charge you to diagnose it, so be sure to find out first.

If you are having issues with a particular component, then you can try to contact the support department for that product. Many times they will be able to give you some ideas of why the part is not working since they should be very familiar with it and have most likely had to deal with the same problem before. If you can't get through on the phone, see if they have an online chat option.

It might be a good idea to see what kind of support is offered with your components from the manufacturer before buying them. If they have free phone support that is the way to go, because email support doesn't help you when you're in a pinch.

Chapter 4 – Putting the Pieces Together

Finally, the time has come to start building your new computer, and hopefully you are excited rather than nervous. It's pretty hard to do any permanent damage unless you get too rough installing components on the motherboard or break off a resistor or capacitor on the motherboard. Just remember to handle things carefully and watch out for that static electricity.

You can build your computer any way you desire to make it easier on yourself, but there are certain steps that I feel should be done in a specific order that will help avoid any unnecessary headaches. If you take things one step at a time rather than trying to do multiple things at once, there will be fewer chances for mistakes.

Assembly Order

Like I just mentioned before, it's up to you to decide how you want to build your computer, but I like to do things in a certain order, and it usually works out well for me when I stick to my game plan.

Figure 4.1

First I will give you a brief rundown on how the components should be installed and then get into more detail in the following sections. Here is the way I like to assemble a computer when building one from scratch:

- Install the processor, heatsink, and fan on the motherboard.
- Connect the processor fan power cable to the motherboard.
- Install the RAM on the motherboard.
- Install the power supply in the case.
- Mount any extra fans in the case.
- Mount the hard drive to its case adapter if required.
- Mount the hard drive and DVD drive in the case.
- Mount the motherboard in the case.
- Connect the case wires to the motherboard.
- Connect any case fan power cables to the motherboard or power supply depending on their connection type.
- Connect the SATA cables to the hard drive and DVD drive and then to the motherboard.
- Install any standalone cards on the motherboard.
- Connect the power cables from the power supply to the motherboard, hard drive, and DVD drive (and standalone\expansion cards if needed).

Installing Components on the Motherboard
I always like to install the processor and RAM on the motherboard before mounting the motherboard in the case. This way I have more room to work in case it's a tight fit, or if I need to look at the bottom of the motherboard to make sure the processor mounts are all the way in.

Installing the Processor\CPU
The process for installing the CPU on the motherboard might vary a little between models and motherboards, but it's the same idea either way. On the motherboard there will be a lever you pull up to open the socket so it will allow you to insert the processor into the socket. If there is a plastic protector plate in there, then you will need to remove that before installing the processor.

Figure 4.2

Then you will insert the processor where the socket protector was, but make sure you put it in the correct way. It will be keyed so it will only go in one way. It's easy to bend the pins if you push down on it if it's not turned the right way, so if it's not just dropping in, then you need to take a closer look at it. Figure 4.3 shows an LGA-1155 processor socket and figure 4.4 shows the bottom of an Intel i7 processor that fits in that socket.

Figure 4.3

Figure 4.4

Once you have the processor resting in the socket, then you will pull the lever back down to secure it in place. It will take a bit of pressure to secure it, but if it's not going down smoothly, then make sure you have everything seated right and try it again.

The fan and heatsink will go on top of the computer and then mount to the motherboard to secure it. Most of the time the fan and heatsink will be one unit, so there will be no assembly required there.

Before mounting the fan\heatsink on top of the processor you will need to apply some thermal paste to the top of the processor. You apply it to the top of the processor and spread it around so it makes a thin layer that covers the entire surface area. This paste is a very high heat conductive material that is used between the processor and heatsink to get better heat conduction and keep the processor cool.

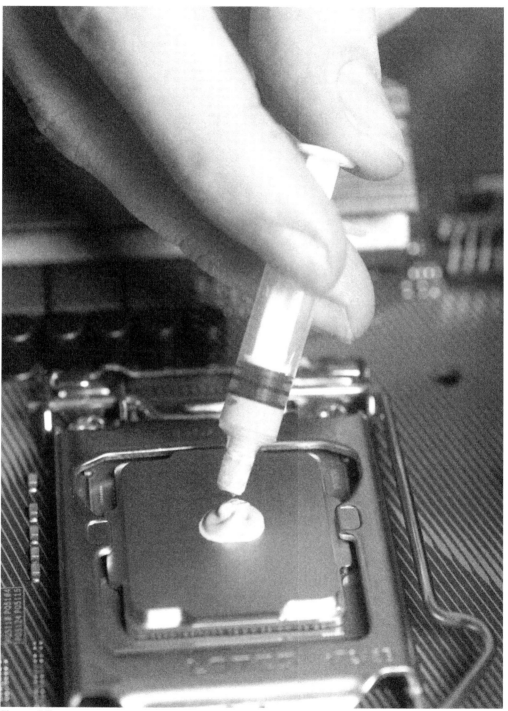

Figure 4.5

Many heatsinks will come with the thermal paste already applied to the bottom of the heatsink (figure 4.6) so you don't have to do this step, so check yours out before going out to get your own paste.

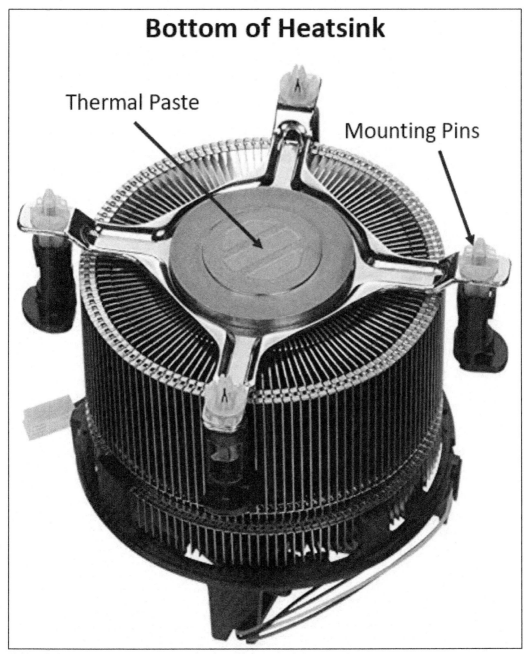

Figure 4.6

Some people don't think the preinstalled paste is good enough, so they will add their own to the top of the processor. I have had good luck with the pre-pasted heatsinks, so it's up to you if you want to take the extra step and add your own.

Next, you will need to mount the fan and heatsink to the motherboard on top of the processor. This process will vary depending on what socket type\processor you are using. Some might have twist lock mounting pins (as seen in figure 4.6), while others might have clips to connect to the motherboard, so you will need to follow the instructions that came with your processor to do this part.

Finally, you will connect the processor fan power wire to the appropriate port on the motherboard. There should be a four pin connector on the motherboard that is labeled CPU Fan or something similar. Don't mistake it for one that says SYS Fan, because those are used for case fans etc.

Figure 4.7

Installing RAM

Installing RAM is a very easy step in the computer building process, but you still need to be careful since you can damage the RAM if you try and insert it the wrong way or force it in.

RAM sticks are notched so they only go in one way. If you take a look at figure 4.8, you will see that the notch is not centered, so one side is longer than the other. Figure 4.8 shows that the two sticks are facing the opposite of each other since the notches don't line up.

Another thing to make a note of is that some RAM sticks will come with exposed circuitry and some will have a cover on them. When handling RAM, be careful where you grab and keep your fingers *off* the gold pins at the bottom that actually go into the RAM slot on the motherboard.

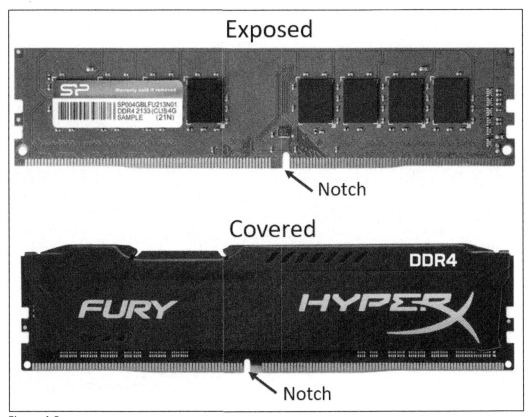

Figure 4.8

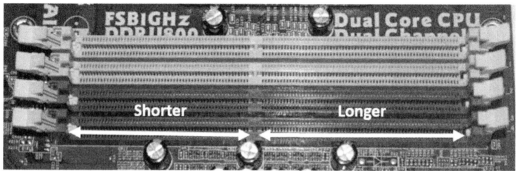

Figure 4.9

Notice the different colored RAM slots in figure 4.9. I mentioned this earlier when talking about dual-channel memory, so make sure you use the right slots. They should be numbered starting with 0 or 1. Check your motherboard manual for their recommendations.

To install the RAM you need to pull back on the retention clips to open them and then insert the stick into the slot at an angle, making sure you have the longer side of the RAM matched up with the longer part of the slot.

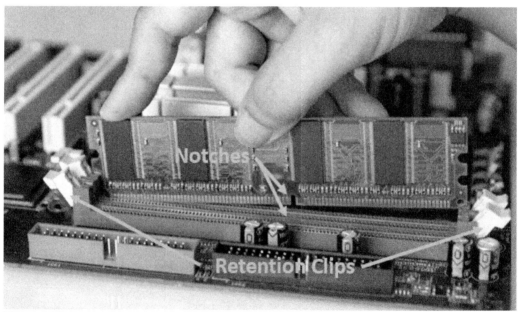

Figure 4.10

Then press down on the stick and it should snap into place and close the retention clip at the same time. It will be pretty obvious if you don't have it inserted all the way because the clip won't be all the way closed.

Installing Components in the Case

Now that you have your motherboard ready to go, it's time to start mounting your components inside the case. If you haven't done so yet, remove the screws that are holding the side of the case in place and then remove the side of the case. Then place the case down on a table so you can see into the open part of the case. Look it over and plan out where you want to install your hard drive and DVD drive since those are pretty much the only parts you will be able to install in more than one place. The inside of your case won't necessarily look like figure 4.11, but you get the basic idea.

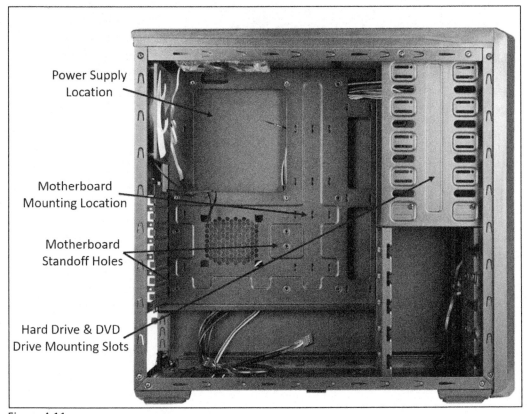

Figure 4.11

Power Supply

I usually start by mounting the power supply first (unless it looks like it will get in the way of mounting the motherboard, then you can do it afterward). By the way, some power supplies will mount at the bottom of the case rather than the top, so don't get confused by figure 4.11 if yours doesn't look the same.

To mount the power supply in the case, slide it in from the inside so the power supply mounting holes line up with the mounting holes in the case. It should only go one way so you can't accidentally mount it upside down.

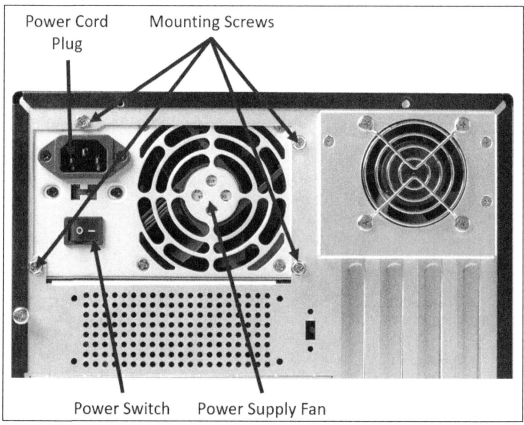

Figure 4.12

Then screw in the four mounting screws to secure the power supply in place. If you have the type of power supply that has removable power cables, don't connect them yet.

Extra Fans
If you plan on installing any extra case fans inside your computer, now is the time to mount them. Make sure they are mounted correctly and facing the right direction so they blow air out of the computer and not suck it in.

You will connect the power for your fan(s) later, so don't worry about it for now. Also make sure that they will not be blocking access to any other devices or where you'll be mounting the motherboard, or else you will have to install them later.

Hard Drive & DVD Drive Installation
Now it's time to figure out where you want your hard drive to go in the case. Since you won't be accessing the hard drive from the outside of the case like you will with the DVD drive, you should mount it where it is out of the way of other devices and the power and SATA connections will be easily accessible. You may have to move it around once you install the rest of the components if something ends up being in the way.

To mount the hard drive you will need to remove the other side of the case so you can use the screws to attach the drive to both sides of the case. Some nicer cases come with hard drive caddies where you mount the hard drive into the caddy and then slide it into the hard drive slot and it locks into place with no screws required to hold it in.

If it's a 3.5 inch hard drive, you should be able to mount it directly in the case. If it's a 2.5 inch drive, you will probably have to use a hard drive adapter (figure 4.14).

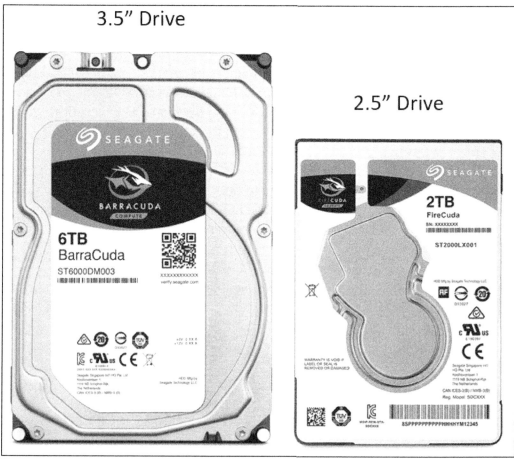

Figure 4.13

Figure 4.14

You only need to use two of the three mounting holes on each side for the hard drive. Simply position the hard drive in the case so the holes line up and use the screws provided with the hard drive to mount it into the case.

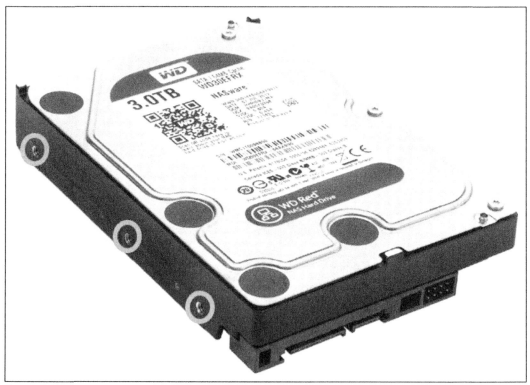

Figure 4.15

Just make sure the SATA and power connection are facing the back of the case so you can get to them to connect them when the time comes. (We will worry about installing the cables once the motherboard is in place.) If it looks like it might be difficult to reach these hard drive connections, then you can connect the cables to the back of the drive before mounting it in place to make things easier.

One exception to this rule is if your case has a removable hard drive mounting bracket, which allows you to mount the hard drive(s) in this bracket outside of the case and then just mount the bracket back in the case afterward (figure 4.16).

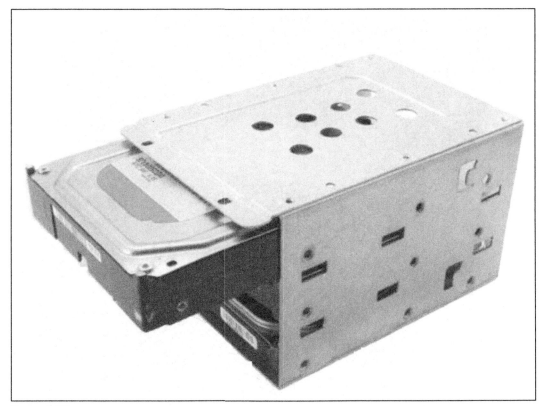

Figure 4.16

The DVD drive mounts in a similar fashion as the hard drive but is larger in size (at 5.25 inches). It will go through the front of the case, and you might have to remove the front case cover to be able to install it. There should be some removable plastic plates on the front of the case, and you will need to pop out the one where you want your DVD drive to go. Most people put the DVD drive near the top of the case.

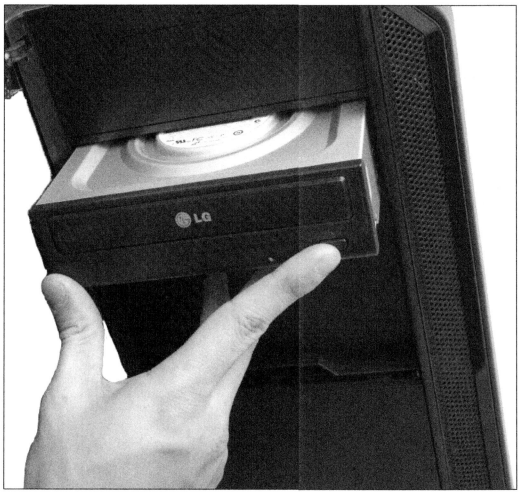

Figure 4.17

Then you will secure the DVD drive with two screws on each side as you did with the hard drive. The same thing applies to the SATA and power cable where you can attach them later, or attach them before inserting the drive if you don't think you will be able to attach them after they are mounted.

Mounting the Motherboard
Now comes the moment of truth—when you finally get to install your shiny new motherboard into its shiny new case. This is when things are finally starting to come together and your parts are starting to look like a computer, but don't rush things! The motherboard has a lot of sensitive components on it that can be easily damaged.

The first thing you want to do is make sure that the holes in the motherboard line up with the holes in the bottom of the case. It's rare that the hole pattern in the case will exactly match the holes in the motherboard, but you should make sure you get enough of them matching up for a secure hold.

Rather than installing a standoff in every hole of the case, I like to see which ones line up and only use those so you don't end up with a standoff pressing against the back of your motherboard.

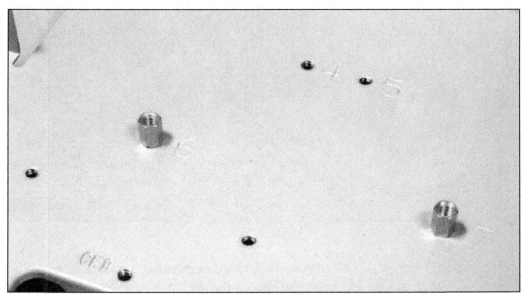

Figure 4.18

Some cases will actually have built in threaded standoffs (figure 4.19) so you don't need to install any at all. The motherboard rests on top of them and you just use the motherboard mounting screws to attach it directly to the case.

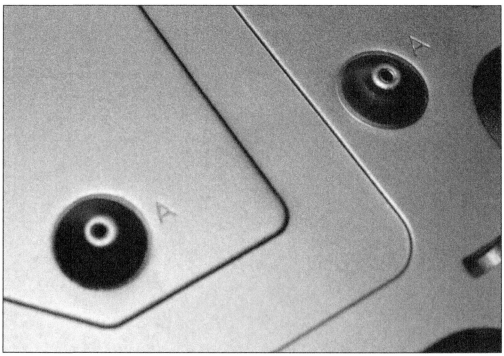

Figure 4.19

Motherboard screws will often come with washers made out of a plastic or a felt-like material that goes between the top of the motherboard and the bottom of the screw head.

Figure 4.20

Once you get the standoffs in place and the holes lined up, then simply screw in your motherboard using the appropriate screws to secure the motherboard to the case. Tighten them until they are snug, but be sure not to overtighten them and break or strip anything.

When you are getting all of your parts together it might be a good idea to get a computer screw kit. This way if you lose any screws or don't have enough of a certain type, you can get a replacement from your kit. They should only run you around $10.

Case\Power Supply Connections and Standalone Cards

Now it's time to get all of your components wired up for connectivity and power. Take your time when doing this so you can have everything neat and organized and don't end up with a rat's nest of tangled up wires and cables. When you are done, you can use your zip ties to make everything look tidy. If you are using any standalone cards such as a PCIe video card, this is the time to install those as well.

Connect the Case Wires to the Motherboard
Your case will have wires connected to it that are used for things such as the power switch, reset button, power LED light, and so on, and these wires need to be connected to their respective place on the motherboard so that you can do things like turn the computer on and see the power and hard drive lights etc.

On the motherboard, look for a group of pins that have labels similar to figure 4.21. Your motherboard manual will tell you where to connect these wires, and the names may or may not match up with my example. Make a note of the + and – signs as well when attaching these wires so you connect them the right way. There is a good chance that you will not have a wire for every connection on the motherboard since some cases are different than others. For example, your case might not have a reset button, yet you might have a place for a reset button connection on your motherboard.

Figure 4.21

There will also be some connections for the front and rear USB connections (assuming you have both), and they will have a spot on the motherboard as well. As you can see from figure 4.22, the USB 2 and USB 3 connections are different, so depending on what type of ports your case has will determine where you make the connections.

USB 2 Header   USB 3 Header

Figure 4.22

There will also be labels for the front and rear USB ports, and how they are labeled will vary depending on your motherboard model. If you look at the USB 3 header in figure 4.22, you will see how it says *F_SUSB3* (the F stands for front). Once again, check your motherboard manual to see what connections you should use for what.

Most cases will come with front audio ports for headphones and a microphone, so you will need to connect the wires from these ports to your motherboard. Most likely the port on the motherboard will say something similar to *F_AUDIO* like shown in figure 4.23

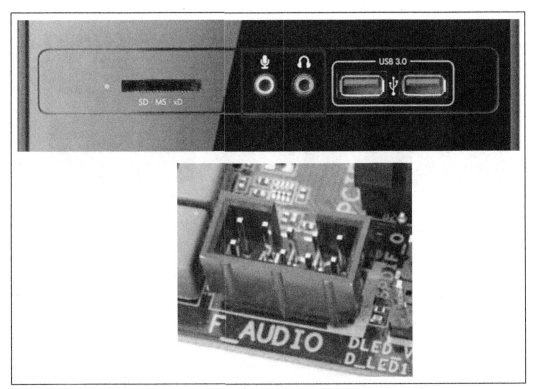

Figure 4.23

Don't forget to attach the power for your case fan(s), otherwise things will be getting hot in a hurry. There are a couple of ways your fan can connect to get its power. It may connect to a port on the motherboard or attach to a power cable coming off of the power supply, so you will need to look at the end and see which type it is. The motherboard connection type will have a three or four female pin connection while the power supply connection will have what is called a Molex connector that plugs into a power cable from the power supply.

Figure 4.24

The connection on the motherboard will have four pins and may be labeled something like SYS_FAN (for system fan) or CHA_FAN (for chassis fan) depending on your motherboard.

Figure 4.25

The three pin fan connector will work with the four pin motherboard connector, but it will only provide power where the four pin fan connectors have the ability to allow the motherboard to control the fan speed as needed.

If your case came with any additional features (such as SD card reader slots), then you will need to connect that cable to the appropriate port on the motherboard. There is a good chance it will just be a USB 2 or 3 connection. If your case didn't come with one of these, then you can easily add one (figure 4.26), and it will install in the case just like your DVD drive does. Just make sure you have a free USB port on the motherboard before adding one of these devices.

Figure 4.26

Connect the SATA Cables to the Motherboard
In order for your hard drive(s) and DVD drive to transfer data (files), you will need to attach them to the motherboard so they can communicate with the computer. This is done via the SATA cables that should have come with your drives or motherboard. If you didn't get these for some reason, you will need to go out and get some.

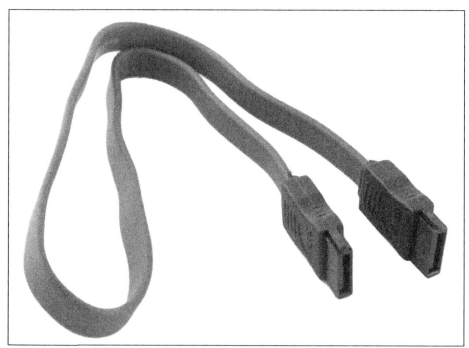

Figure 4.27

Before going any further I just want to quickly go over the SATA versions so you know how things have changed throughout the years. There are currently three versions of SATA called SATA1, SATA2, and SATA3, with SATA3 currently being used by modern SATA devices. There are several revisions within each one, but I will only list the ones that pertain to speed.

- **SATA1** – The first generation of SATA that transfers data at a speed of 1.5Gbps.

- **SATA2** – The second generation of SATA that transfers data at a speed of 3Gbps.

- **SATA3** – The third generation of SATA that transfers data at a speed of 6Gbps. Revision 3.2, which is known as SATAe (for express), offers speeds of 16Gbps. There is even a revision 3.5 that offers even higher performance.

Most likely your new devices will be SATA3 rated, but double check to make sure you aren't getting some old leftover hardware. As for the cables, you should be able to use SATA2 or SATA3 cables interchangeably and the speed will be the same. The only difference between the two cables is the SATA3 cable will have locking clips on them (figure 4.28).

Figure 4.28

Now you can connect one end of your SATA cable to your hard drive and the other to a SATA port on the motherboard. Just remember what I mentioned back in Chapter 2 about finding out which port is the primary SATA port and use that for the hard drive you will be using for your operating system. They should be different colors and also labeled on the motherboard, so you can then check the motherboard manual to see which port is used for what.

Before you start making your motherboard connections, it a good idea to look at the diagram that should be in your motherboard manual. This way you can get an idea of where all the connections are on the motherboard so you are not hunting for them while trying to make the connections.

Figure 4.29

Standalone\Expansion Card Installation
I've talked about how motherboards will have built in video, audio, and network, so there is no need to have a standalone version of any of these devices unless you need additional capabilities that the built in version can't provide. The most common standalone card to buy is a video card, especially for gamers.

To install your standalone card, choose the appropriate slot (most likely a PCIe slot) and carefully insert the card into the slot, making sure you are doing it in the right direction. There are removable panels on the back of the case and you'll need to remove the one that lines up with the slot on the motherboard you are planning to use for your card. This way the back of the card will be accessible from the back of the case.

There will be some screws on the inside of the case that you can remove to take out the expansion card cover panel so it will fit through the back of the case (figure

4.30). Some cases might not have screws, and have some kind of clip that you will undo instead. With cheaper cases, you might find yourself having to pry them out and pretty much break them off.

Figure 4.30

Once you have everything ready to go, simply install the expansion card in the slot like you did when installing your RAM, making sure the slots in the card line up with the slot you are inserting the card into. Some cards will go in easier at an angle while others will go in easier straight down. You will also notice that there is a clip on the expansion slot that helps to keep the card in place.

Figure 4.31

After the card is properly inserted, use the screw from the expansion card case cover to secure the top of the card to the case (figure 4.32). It will screw into the same hole that the cover used.

Figure 4.32

Connect the Power Cables
The final step in the assembly process is to attach all of the power connections from the power supply to the motherboard, drives, and anything else that needs power. Be sure to make sure the switch on the back of the power supply is turned off before connecting any power. (It should have been off for the entire build, of course.)

The order that you connect your components is up to you, but I will now go over the things that need to be connected to the power supply.

Connect the 24 pin motherboard power connector to the motherboard. It will only go in one direction, so you can't get it wrong.

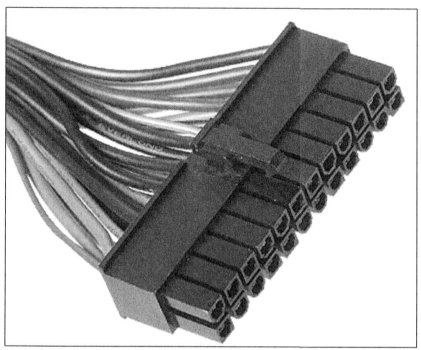

Figure 4.33

Figure 4.34

There will also be a four pin or eight pin CPU power connection on the motherboard depending on your motherboard model (as I discussed back in Chapter 2 when I talked about power supplies). You will need to connect this to the motherboard as well. Your manual should have a diagram of where all the specific connections are located on the motherboard.

To connect the power to your SATA hard drive and DVD drive, locate a SATA power cable (as shown in figure 4.35) and attach it to the SATA power connector on the hard drive or DVD drive (as shown in figure 4.36).

Figure 4.35

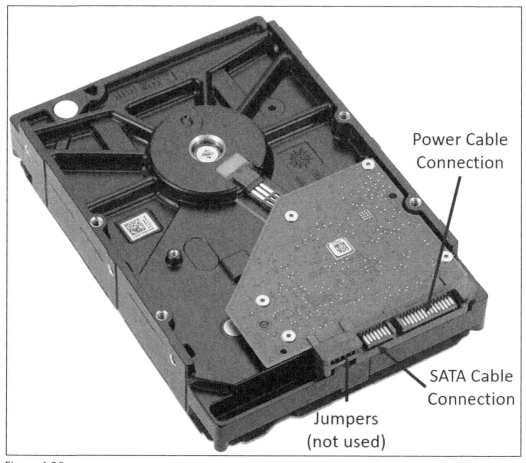

Figure 4.36

The connector is keyed like an L shape and will only go on in one direction so you can't get it backwards. If you notice an area with eight pins showing, that is for setting jumpers, which is not something you will generally need to worry about.

High end video cards will have their own power connection since they need more power than the PCIe slot can provide them with to run properly. Figure 4.37 shows a video card with two 8 pin power connections and one 6 pin power connection. Check with the video card documentation to see which power cables they recommend you connect.

Figure 4.37

The 6 pin connector can provide up to 75 watts while the 8 pin connector can provide up to 150 watts, but not all video cards require the same amount of power. High end video cards are another reason why you need to have a power supply with a higher output so you can properly power them.

Chapter 5 – Initial Power Up

With all of the components in place and everything wired and cabled up correctly, it's time to press the power button and hopefully watch the computer come to life. Of course, first you should double check all of your connections to make sure everything is where it is supposed to be, and now is the time to turn the switch on the back of the power supply from off to on, otherwise you won't be getting too far at all.

Make sure to connect your monitor, keyboard, and mouse to the computer *before* powering it up, otherwise you won't be able to see or do anything. If you have a wireless mouse and keyboard, then there will be a chance it won't work, so I always like to use a USB mouse and keyboard for the first power up and also to install the operating system.

This chapter will focus on what happens when you first power up your computer and what you should be looking for and adjusting before you go on to the next step, which is installing your operating system. If everything works out okay, then this should be a pretty quick process.

What to Expect

The first thing to expect when you press the power button is that the computer itself turns on. You should hear the power supply fan spinning and also see the CPU and case fans spinning if you still have the cover off (which I recommend doing so you can spot any problems such as wires getting caught in a fan etc.). Now is the time to make sure you mounted your extra case fans the right way, too.

Depending on the type of hard drive you have, you might hear it spin up as well if it's a SATA drive with moving parts. Some SATA drives are super quiet and hard to hear. Since there are no moving parts in an SSD drive, then you most likely won't hear a peep from it. If you take a look at the HDD light on the front of the case, you might see it flashing randomly. You should also see your power LED light on the front of the case come on.

You should see something appear on your monitor pretty quickly after powering up your computer. Depending on the make and model of your motherboard, you might see something similar to figure 5.1 but if you have a newer computer then will probably look different or go by so fast that you don't see anything.

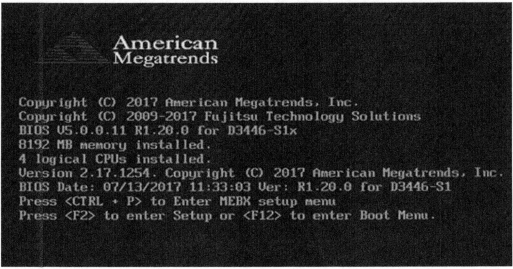

Figure 5.1

This is called a POST screen, which stands for Power On Self-Test. During this process, the motherboard goes through its configuration and checks things such as the amount of installed memory, selecting and initializing bootable devices, checking for an attached keyboard, and so on. If something is not right, then it will stop the boot process and give you an error message or a series of beeps indicating what the problem is.

If everything is okay, then it will try and find a device to boot from and fail because you don't have an operating system set up yet. You will get a message similar to figure 5.2, and the computer won't go any further than that until you install your operating system, which I will cover in the next chapter.

Some motherboards have the POST screen hidden on startup so you don't see the status as the computer is booting up. Often it will show the manufacturers "splash screen" logo instead. There may or may not be an option in the settings to enable the POST screen to display on startup.

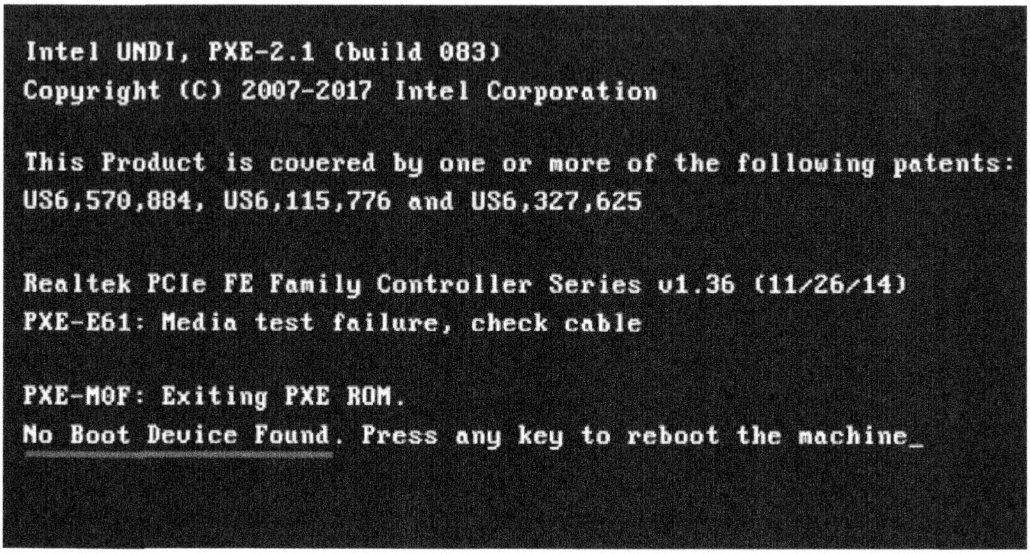

```
Intel UNDI, PXE-2.1 (build 083)
Copyright (C) 2007-2017 Intel Corporation

This Product is covered by one or more of the following patents:
US6,570,884, US6,115,776 and US6,327,625


Realtek PCIe FE Family Controller Series v1.36 (11/26/14)
PXE-E61: Media test failure, check cable


PXE-M0F: Exiting PXE ROM.
No Boot Device Found. Press any key to reboot the machine_
```

Figure 5.2

Accessing the BIOS\UEFI Settings

All motherboards will have a built-in BIOS (Basic Input Output System) or the newer UEFI (Unified Extensible Firmware Interface), and both of these are used as a software interface between an operating system and the platform firmware. Yours should come with a UEFI since using a BIOS went out a few years ago, but keep in mind that if you are working on an older computer, you will be accessing the BIOS rather than UEFI to check settings and change system configurations. Figure 5.3 shows a typical BIOS screen while figure 5.4 shows a UEFI screen, which you can see looks much more modern than the older version.

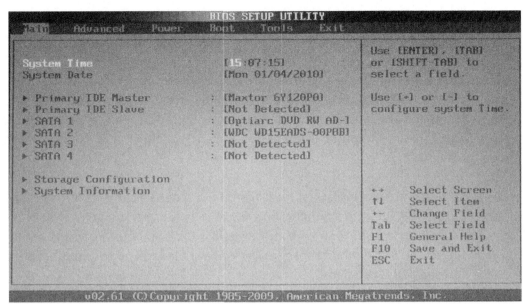

Figure 5.3

Figure 5.4

Most UEFI interfaces will also allow you to use the mouse where the older BIOS screens are menu driven (using the arrow keys and Enter button on the keyboard).

There are other benefits of UEFI over BIOS, but you can check that out yourself if you are interested in learning more.

The main reason you would go into either of these interfaces is to make sure that your hardware is being recognized accurately by the computer. You can check things like your RAM capacity and hard drive configuration, as well as change the boot order of your computer if needed. You can also check and set the system time from here.

To get to these settings, look for a message on the screen during startup that says press "x" to enter setup or configuration etc. It may be something like the delete or escape key, or maybe one of the F keys like F2. Your motherboard manual should tell you how to get into these settings or you can look up your motherboard online and see if you can find it.

Once you are in there, you can browse around and look at all the specific settings. I wouldn't recommend changing any of them unless you know what you are doing or if there is a real need to do so. In most cases when you exit the BIOS or UEFI, it will ask you if you want to save your changes, so if you *did* do something by accident simply say *no* to saving any changes. Once you exit, it will most likely go back to the *no operating system found* screen, and there is not much you can do except install an operating system (which is covered in the next chapter).

Troubleshooting a Blank Screen or No Power
Hopefully you will never have to deal with this problem, but sometimes when you turn on your computer for the first time you will get a blank screen. This can be frustrating because you will not get any error message, and probably not any error beep codes either.

No Power
If you press the power button on your new computer and nothing happens at all, then there are some things you can do to try and troubleshoot the problem. Sometimes it's an easy fix, and other times it can be frustrating and require some serious troubleshooting.

The obvious things to check, of course, is that the computer is plugged into the wall and that the power cord is securely plugged into the back of the power supply. If you have another power cable, you can replace it to rule out a faulty cable. Many monitor power cables are the same type, so you can try that if that's the case with your monitor. Also, be sure that the on\off switch on the back of the power supply is switched to on. Sometimes it's hard to tell which way is on and which way is off.

Next, you can check the power connection from the power supply to the motherboard. Make sure it's plugged in correctly and securely (unplug the computer from the wall first). If you have the type of power supply that has removable power cables, then you can try a different cable or a different connection on the motherboard.

Also, take a look at where the power switch wire from the case connects to the motherboard and make sure it's in the right place and connected the right way. The wire should say something like PWR or even POWER on it so you know you are using the right one. There is a way to bypass the power button on the case by taking a small flathead screwdriver and "shorting" the connection between the two pins where the wire connects. In other words, touch both of the pins at the same time with the screwdriver while the computer is plugged in to see if it turns on. If that's the case, you have a bad power button or power wire in your case.

Figure 5.5

If you still can't get it to power up, then you might be looking at a bad power supply or even a dead motherboard. I have had to exchange the motherboard a few times on computer builds because they were simply no good. The power supply would be easier to replace first as a test. You can also take the computer down to a shop and have the power tested (unless you have your own test equipment on hand).

Blank Screen

So let's say your new computer actually turns on and you can hear the fans moving, but you don't see anything on the screen. There are some basic things you can check to troubleshoot this type of problem.

The first thing is to check the obvious, like checking to see if the video cable is securely attached to the computer and monitor at both ends. Also, check for any bent pins on the video cable or try another one if you happen to have one.

If your video card has different types of outputs (such as a VGA and HDMI connection) then try a different connection to see if that does anything. Of course, your monitor will have to support the other type of connection as well. You can always use your TV as a monitor if needed if it has the right type of connection.

What you can do next is to make sure everything is connected properly and securely. Just be sure to turn off the computer and unplug it first. You don't want to ruin your new computer before you even figure out what the problem is!

If you have a standalone video card, make sure it is seated properly in the slot or even take it out and reinstall it. You can also try a different PCIe slot as a test. If that doesn't work, then try to use one of the video ports on the built-in video card. It may be a case that you need to make a change in your BIOS\UEFI settings so the motherboard knows to use the standalone video card.

Also, try to reseat your RAM since that can cause the same problem. If you have more than one stick, you can try removing one and try to turn on your computer with only one installed. If you still don't see anything on the screen, then try the same thing with the other stick or try different RAM slots altogether.

If your processor is not working correctly, then it will also cause the computer not to display any video. It's kind of a pain, but you might want to remove the processor and check for any bent pins on the bottom of the processor or on the socket (depending on what processor you are using). If you do see a bent pin, it is possible to straighten it out if you do it very carefully with some small needle nose pliers or a tweezer.

If nothing seems to work, then it might be a case of a faulty motherboard. I would then call the support number for your motherboard manufacturer and see if they have some other tests they can have you run, or they might just have to replace it for you unless you would rather just take it back to the store where you bought it and exchange it.

Chapter 6 – Installing Your Operating System

Now that you have your new computer assembled and everything is working as it should (hopefully), it's time to make some use of all of those expensive parts. A computer needs to have an operating system (OS) in order to really be used for anything productive. The operating system allows you to install your software and also works with your hardware, allowing it to interface with that software.

Operating systems can be installed using media such as a CD, DVD, or flash drive, and can also be installed over a network. For a home user, you will most likely use one of the first three options, and typically won't be installing your OS over a network. To use a CD, DVD, or flash drive, you simply insert it in the drive, power up the computer, and follow the prompts. In order to do that, the computer will need to know to check your CD\DVD drive or USB ports for OS installation media. By default, the computer will usually read from the hard drive first and will give you an error such as *no operating system found* since you haven't installed one yet.

Changing the Boot Order
As I mentioned in Chapter 5, you can access the BIOS\UEFI Settings when booting your computer and change the boot order so it uses a different device to boot from, or to try to boot from first. Some computers will try the other devices in the computer to boot from if they can't boot from the hard drive while others will just stop after checking the first one on the list.

If your computer is not reading your CD\DVD or USB drives, then you might need to go into the BIOS\UEFI settings and change the boot order. To get to your BIOS\UEFI settings, start your computer and look for what it says you need to do to enter setup. You may have to press something like the delete, ESC, or F2 key to get into your BIOS\UEFI. Not all systems are the same, but your computer should tell you what key to press to enter setup when booting your computer. If not, then many times you can press one or more of these keys over and over as the computer is booting and see if you get lucky. Or you can look up your make and model online and see if you can find the right key to press.

Once you get into the BIOS\UEFI, there will most likely be a section named Boot. From there you can change which drive the system looks at first to boot from. Figures 6.1 and 6.2 show a couple of examples of boot order screens from different BIOS\UEFI manufacturers, with figure 6.2 showing the older style that is not really used on newer computers anymore.

Figure 6.1

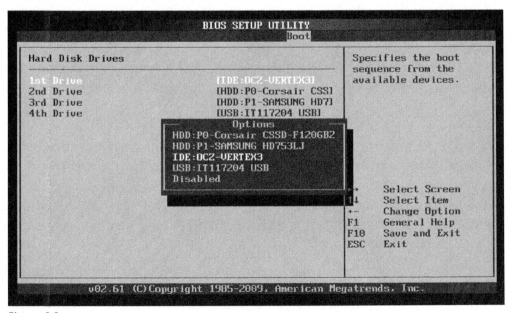

Figure 6.2

Once you set the boot order to the way you want it, make sure to save it before you exit. Most of the time there is a save and exit option where you can do both at once. Then the computer will reboot and read from the new boot device that you chose in the BIOS\UEFI settings. (Keep in mind that this new device will continue to be the boot device until you go back into the BIOS\UEFI and change it back to the way it originally was.)

Another thing to look for is that some computers will show a message saying something like *press F12 to choose boot device*, and if that's the case, you won't need to go into the BIOS\UEFI and change the settings. Then the next time you reboot the computer, it will use its default boot device which should be the hard drive.

Making a Bootable Flash Drive
For the longest time, it has been the norm to install operating systems and other software from CDs and DVDs. Now everything is online, and eventually the CD\DVD drive will go the way of the floppy disk drive—if you even remember those!

While there are several ways to install an operating system on your computer, one way that many people like to use is to install the OS from a bootable USB flash drive. This way they don't need the actual installation CD or DVD, and if they don't have a CD\DVD drive then they can still install the OS.

When you download an operating system image from the Internet it will most likely come in the form of an ISO file. Think of an ISO file kind of like a zip file where you have many files contained within one file. ISO files can be converted into bootable CDs, DVDs, or even flash drives that can be used to start your computer with.

But what if you want to create a bootable flash drive but only have the CD\DVD version of the operating system? Well, one thing you can do is convert the contents of that CD or DVD to an ISO file which can then be used to make a bootable USB flash drive. There are many ways to do this, but I will go over one program that I like to use called ImgBurn. It's a free download and very easy to use. (*http://www.imgburn.com/*)

Once you install ImgBurn and run it, you will see the main menu as shown in figure 6.3. From there you will insert your CD or DVD into your drive and click on *Create image file from disk*.

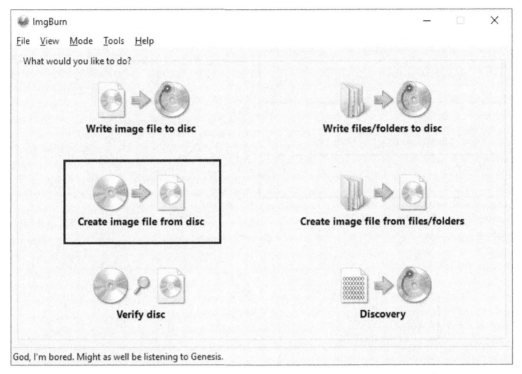

Figure 6.3

Next, you will need to make a couple of selections before creating your ISO file. One thing you need to do is select the source of the files that will be used to create the ISO file, which will be your CD\DVD drive. The other thing you need to do is decide what you want the ISO file to be named and where you want it created. Then, when you are ready to go, simply click on the CD to file button at the bottom of the window.

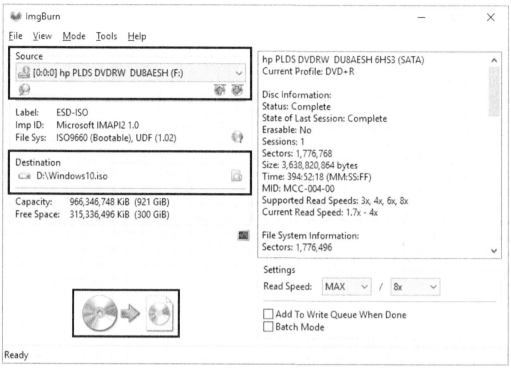

Figure 6.4

ImgBurn will go through the conversion procedure and show you a status bar letting you know how far the process has completed.

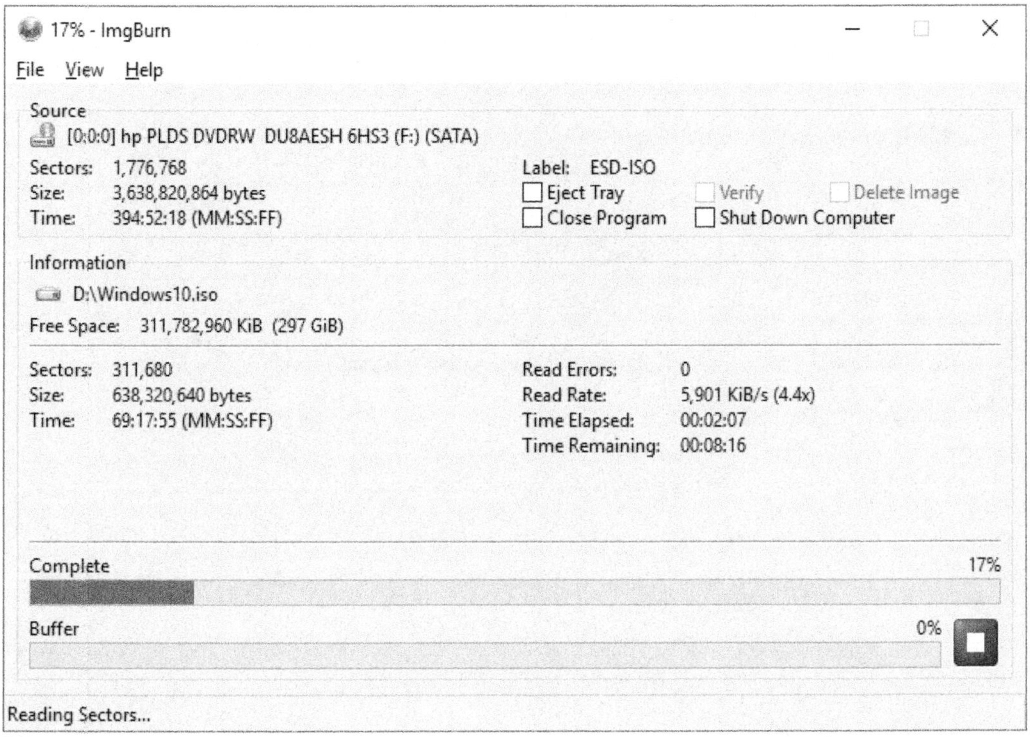

Figure 6.5

When it's complete, it will pop up a message saying *Operation Successfully Completed,* and you can then click *OK* and close the program.

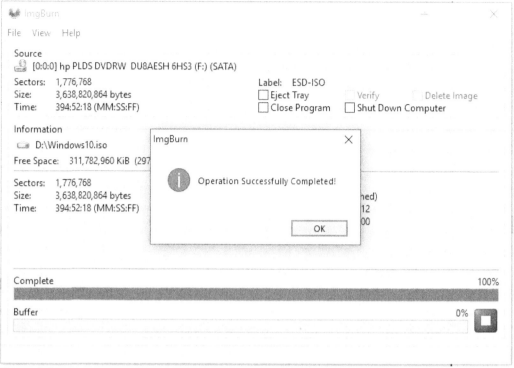

Figure 6.6

Now if you browse to where you told ImgBurn to create the ISO file, you will find it there. You are now ready to create your bootable USB flash drive.

For the creation of the bootable USB flash drive, I will show you a very popular method using a free program that is available to download from the Internet. I will also be using Windows 10 for my ISO image for the bootable flash drive.

Rufus Bootable USB Flash Drive Utility
Rufus is a free utility that will make a USB flash drive bootable, allowing you to boot your computer off of that flash drive like it was a bootable CD or DVD. Rufus can be used with Windows, Linux, and other operating systems that can boot off of an ISO file. All you need to do to get things going is to have your USB drive in your computer and have your ISO file on your computer where you can get to it. Then you will run the Rufus executable file that you downloaded, and then you will be able to customize your settings depending on what type of computer you are attempting to boot if needed.

If you take a look at figure 6.7, you will see that I am using a flash drive that is currently the S: drive on my computer. It's 32GB in size and doesn't have a drive label. If you have more than one flash drive connected to your computer, make sure you select the one you actually want to use to avoid data loss on the one you don't want to use. Or, better yet, remove any other flash drives to avoid any potential confusion.

The ISO file I have selected to use to create the bootable flash drive is called *Windows10Pro.iso* and is stored on my local hard drive. For the volume label name to be used after the bootable flash drive is created I will use *Windows10.* The rest of the options will be selected for you depending on the type of flash drive you are using and the ISO file you will be creating the drive from, even though you can customize them to suit your needs. There are also advanced options for the *Drive Properties* and *Format Options* sections that you can change if needed.

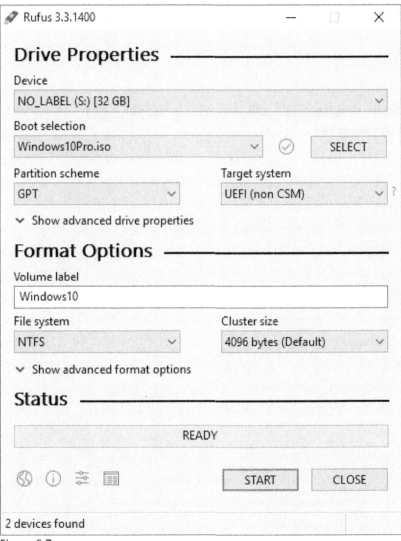

Figure 6.7

When you have everything set, click on the Start button and you will get a warning telling you that everything on the flash drive will be destroyed before creating the new bootable flash drive. So, if you are sure you don't need any data off of the flash drive, click the OK button.

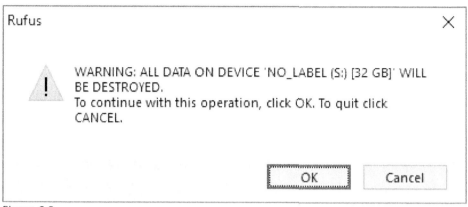

Figure 6.8

Then Rufus will do its thing and you will see what is happening on the status bar at the bottom of the window.

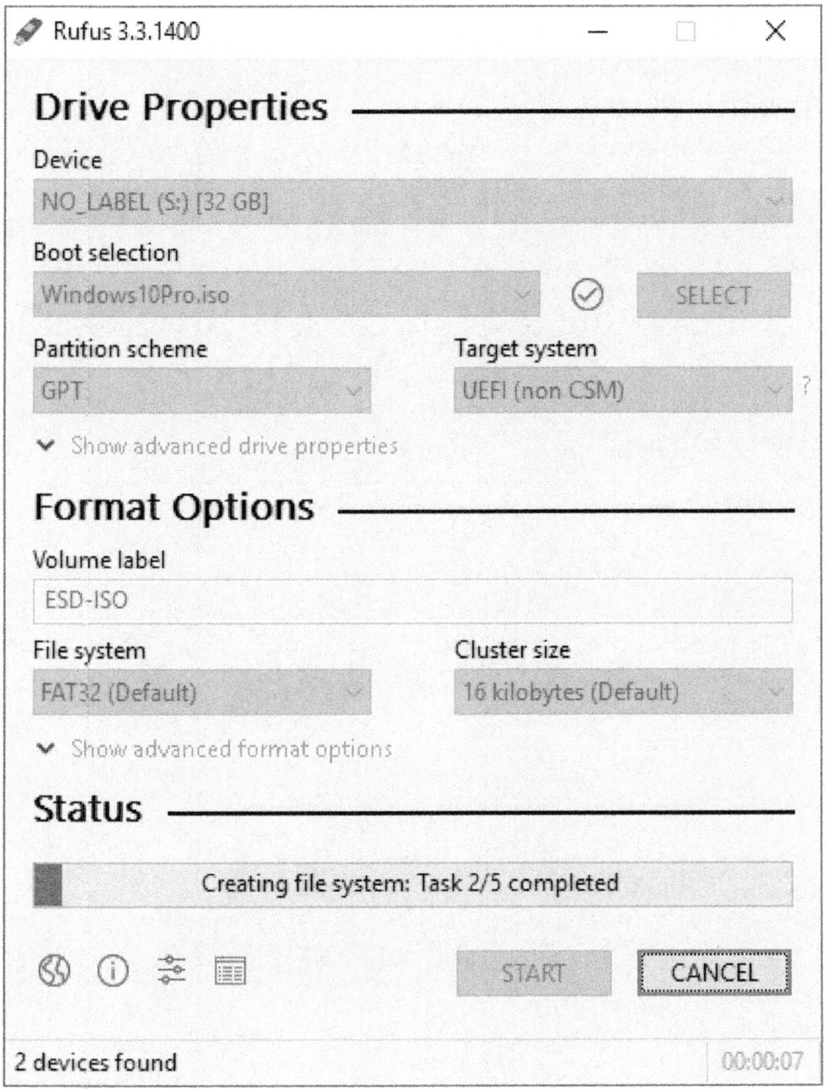

Figure 6.9

When the process is complete it will say READY in the status bar, which can be a little confusing because it doesn't say complete or finished, but it's actually done. Simply click on CLOSE and remove the USB drive from the computer.

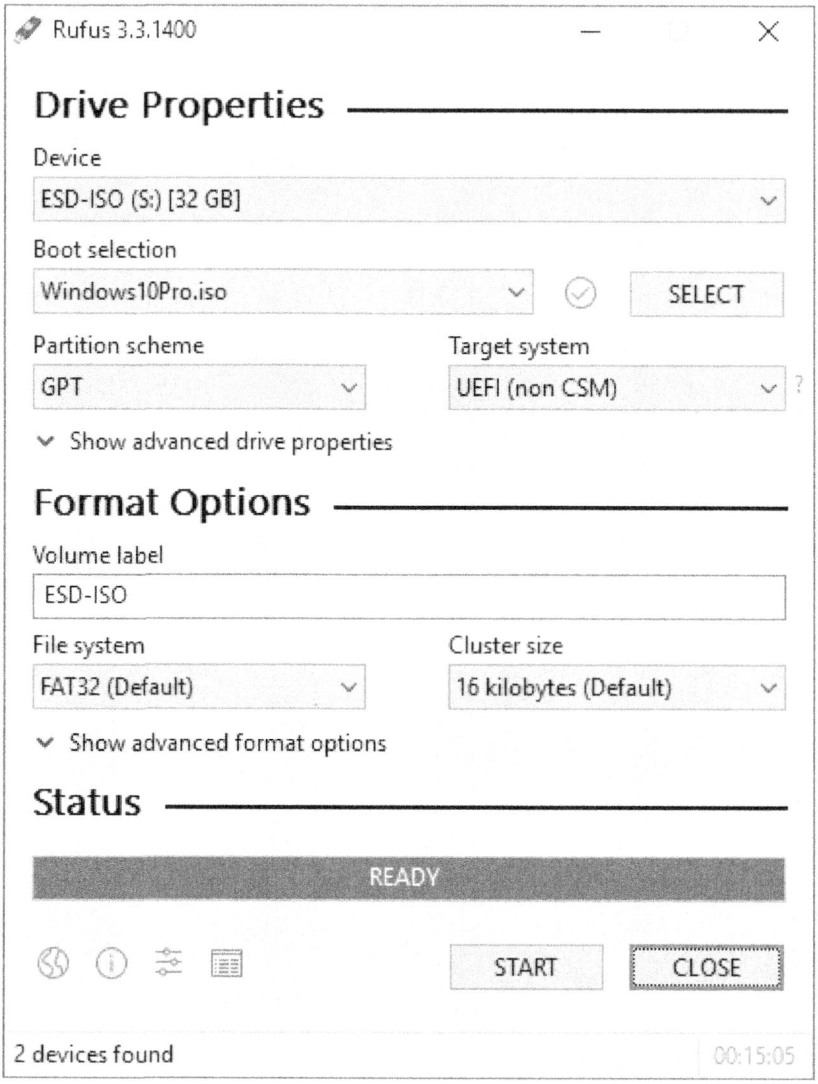

Figure 6.10

Now you will have your bootable flash drive ready to go for your operating system installation. Rufus can be downloaded for free from their website. https://rufus.ie

Installing Windows

If you plan on running Microsoft Windows on your computer, then fortunately the process for installing Windows is pretty simple. I will now go over the steps to perform a clean installation of Windows 11 Home Edition. You can perform an upgrade from within Windows or from booting to the Windows DVD or a bootable flash drive, but for a clean installation, you will want to boot from the Windows

DVD (or flash drive) to start the installation process. If your computer is not set to read from your CD\DVD drive first, then you will need to either go into the BIOS (or UEFI for newer computers) and change the boot order or look for the key that needs to be pressed on startup that will let you choose the boot device. Some computers make it obvious while others don't give you that information. Many times, it's the F12, F2 or Esc key.

If your computer didn't come with a Windows DVD then you should be able to download what they call an ISO file from the Microsoft website and then use your DVD burning software to convert\burn it to a bootable DVD, or even a bootable flash drive.

Once you have booted your computer with your Windows DVD and pressed any key on your keyboard to boot from the DVD, you will be asked to choose your language, time and currency format, and keyboard input. Normally the defaults will be correct, and you can then click on *Next* and then on the *Install now* button.

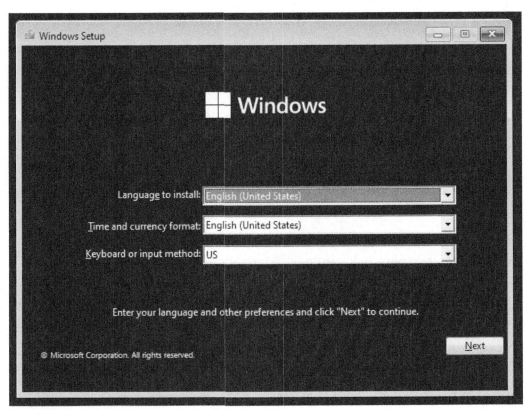

Figure 6.11

On the next screen you will be asked to type in your Windows product key, which will be included with the Windows 11 DVD. If you are using a DVD that you borrowed from someone and your computer originally came with Windows 11, then you can enter the product key from the sticker that should be someplace on your computer's case. If you don't have a key, you can still install Windows by clicking on *I don't have a product key* and then enter one later or use it in trial mode.

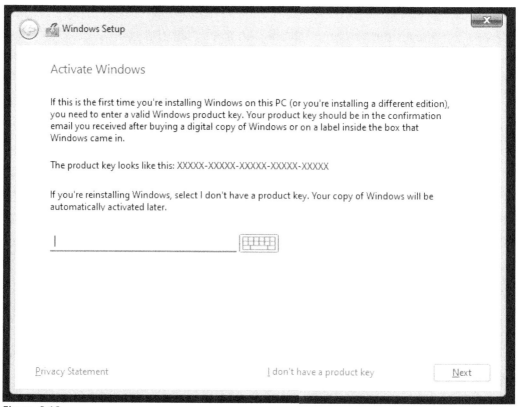

Figure 6.12

Next, you will be able to choose which edition of Windows you want to install. The choices you see here will vary depending on your installation media. Just make sure to choose the one that matches your product key. If you entered the product key, then you might not see this screen because it will choose the edition for you based on that key.

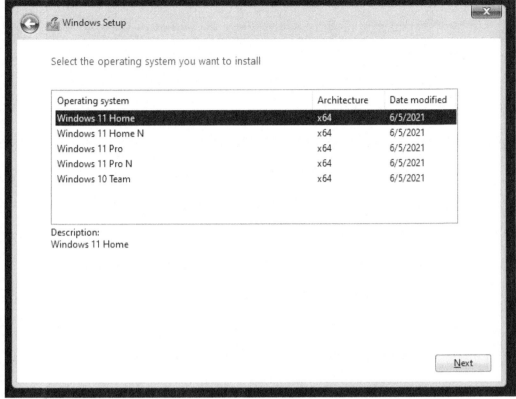

Figure 6.13

Next, you will check the box that says you accept the license terms that are listed. Most people don't read them, but you can if you are feeling up to it!

The next window is where you will have to make a choice based on what type of installation you are doing. Since we are doing a clean installation, we will pick the second option that says *Custom: Install Windows only (advanced)*. You will notice in the description that it says that your files, settings, and applications will not be moved to Windows with this option, so make sure you back up your files!

When installing a clean version of Windows on your existing computer another thing to remember is that you will need to reinstall any programs that don't come with Windows, so make sure you have your installation media for your software.

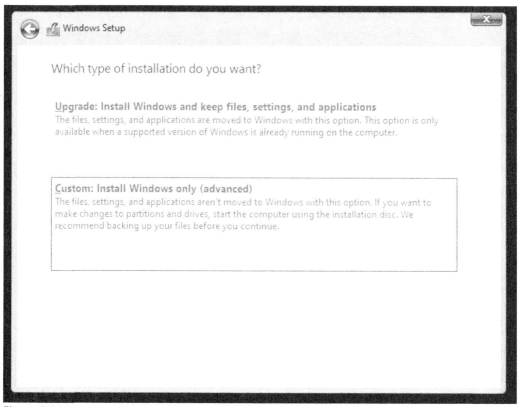

Figure 6.14

The next section is where you will need to choose what hard drive you are going to install Windows 11 on, as well as how much of the hard drive you are going to use. If you click on *Next*, it will use the selected hard drive and create a partition using all the space on the drive. Then it will format the drive to get it ready to install Windows on.

If you click on *New*, then you can decide how much of the total drive capacity will be used for Windows. Then the rest will be listed as "unused", and you can create additional drives with it after Windows is installed.

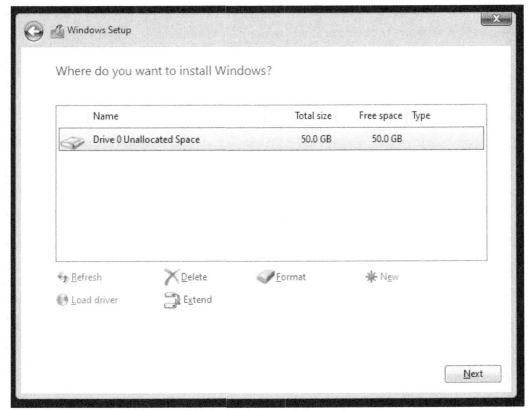

Figure 6.15

Now you can see in figure 6.16 that the installation is running. This process will take a bit of time depending on the performance of the hardware installed in your computer such as processor speed, hard drive type, and the amount of RAM installed.

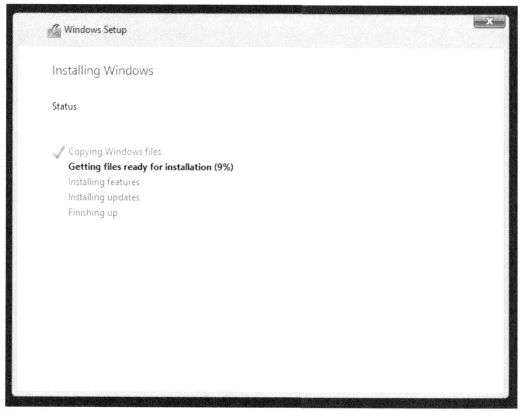

Figure 6.16

After the installation is complete, Windows will restart the computer and prepare your hardware for use with Windows. Then Windows will start up and begin its basic configuration where it will ask you to specify your region, keyboard layout, network (Internet\wireless) connection settings, and will then check for updates.

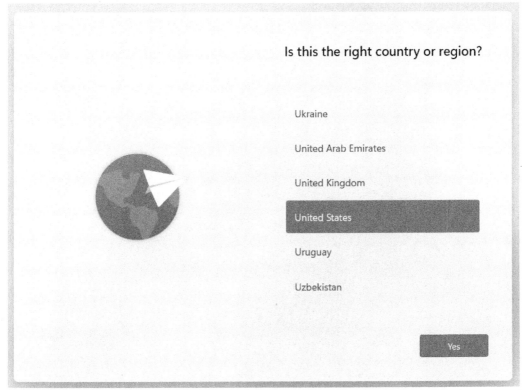

Figure 6.17

At the end will ask you to add your Microsoft account information to your new Windows installation to be used for login purposes. If you don't have a Microsoft account, you can create one from this screen by clicking on the *Create one* link. If you forgot your Microsoft account email or password, you can click on the *Sign-in options* link to go through the reset process.

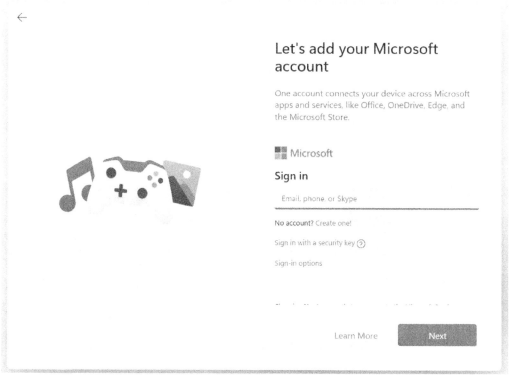

Figure 6.18

Next, you will be prompted to create a PIN that will be used to log into your computer, so you don't need to enter your Microsoft account email address and password each time. This PIN can be something simple such as 4 numbers or you can even add text to make it more like an actual password.

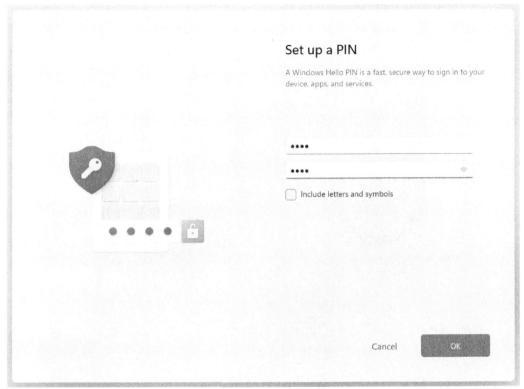

Figure 6.19

Once you are logged in, Windows might ask you if you wish to copy your files and settings from your old computer to your new one, assuming your old computer is not too old and was configured to use OneDrive etc. (figure 6.20).

OneDrive is Microsoft's online cloud storage service that you get for free with Windows. You get a limited amount of online storage space and if you want to get extra then you will have to sign up for one of their subscription plans.

If you are interested in learning more about Microsoft OneDrive and other online cloud platforms such as DropBox and Google Drive, then check out my book titled **Cloud Storage Made Easy**. https://www.amazon.com/dp/1730838359

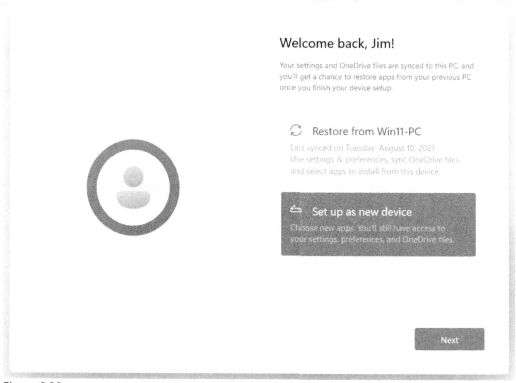

Figure 6.20

I'm going to choose the *Setup as a new device* option and click on the *Next* button. Then you will be prompted to choose your privacy settings and then disable any settings you don't agree with. Generally, I disable all of these settings since Microsoft doesn't need to know what I'm doing on my computer.

After clicking on *Accept* I will then be prompted to let Windows know what I will be doing with my computer so it can "customize my experience". I can also choose the *Skip* button if I don't want Windows to apply any customization.

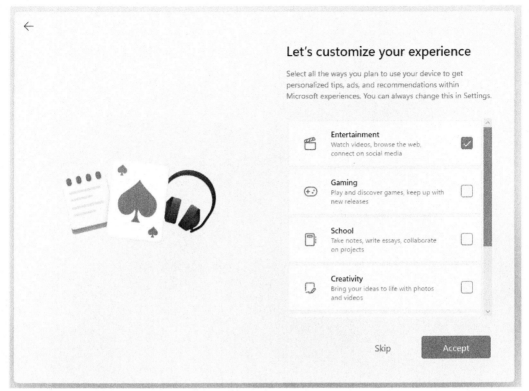

Figure 6.21

Now I will be asked if I want to use OneDrive to back up my files automatically or whether I would like it to be disabled. OneDrive will back up my desktop, documents and pictures folders by default. You can always go back and enable OneDrive if you don't want to use it right away.

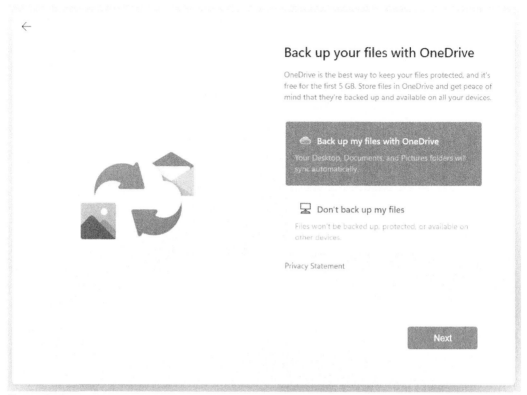

Figure 6.22

After you click on Next, Windows will check for some updates once again and this process can take quite a bit of time to complete. It will also reboot your computer once the updates are complete.

Then you will be asked to enter the PIN you created during the installation process and then Windows will go through a few more setup steps. After that, you will be presented with your new Windows 11 desktop and you will be ready to start using your new operating system.

Windows Update
One last thing I want to mention in this chapter is Windows Update, and what these updates do to your computer. Windows Updates consist of fixes, patches, and upgrades that are applied to your computer to fix bugs, patch security holes, and add new features to Windows. If your computer is connected to the Internet, then these updates are downloaded and installed automatically.

One downside to the way Windows does its updates is that you can't stop them from being installed like you could with previous versions of Windows. Also, if you are not in front of your computer to stop the reboots that are required after many of these updates, then you might lose any unsaved documents that you have open during the reboot. (It's always a good idea to save your work before walking away from your computer for an extended period of time.)

You can view the Windows Update settings and update history from the Windows settings under the Windows Update section. You can click on *Change active hours* in the *Advanced* settings to tell Windows what time period you are active on your computer so it won't automatically restart it during that time period (figure 6.23). You can choose a time span of up to 18 hours.

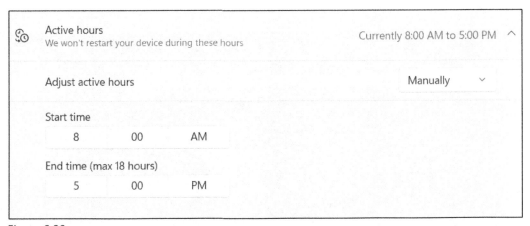

Figure 6.23

Installing Linux

For you non-conformists who want to stay away from Windows and tend to be more on the "techy" side, you can install Linux on your new computer instead. Linux is a free (for the most part), open source operating system that can be downloaded and then installed on your computer.

There are many flavors (versions) of Linux developed by different people that you can choose from. Some are more popular than others, and some will have advantages over the others depending on what you plan to use your computer for. So, if you want to give Linux a try, you should check out some of the flavors and decide what version you want to install.

For my demonstration, I am going to use Ubuntu Linux Desktop since it is very popular and is easier to use for beginners. You can download it for free from their website as a 3.5GB ISO file. They also offer server, developer, and cloud versions of the operating system. Here are the requirements for Ubuntu Linux as of the writing of this book:

(https://www.ubuntu.com/download/desktop).

- 2 GHz dual core processor or better
- 4 GB system memory
- 25 GB of free hard drive space
- Either a DVD drive or a USB port for the installer media

Once you boot your computer with the Ubuntu DVD or flash drive, you will see a screen similar to figure 6.24 and you will need to select the *Try or install Ubuntu* option.

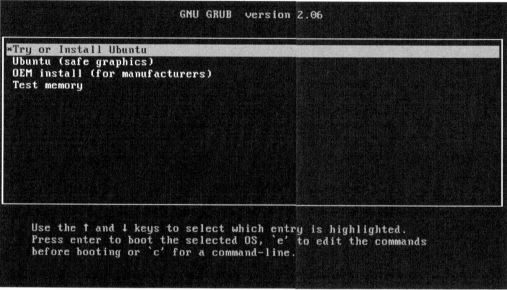

Figure 6.24

The Linux installation is pretty straightforward just like the Windows installation but there are definitely some differences to be aware of.

One big difference is that you can run Ubuntu from the CD without installing it on your computer to see if you like it or not. This works by loading the OS into RAM and running it from there. The downside to this is once you shut down the VM, any changes you made to the OS will be lost. So on that note, I will choose the Install Ubuntu option on my virtual hard disk.

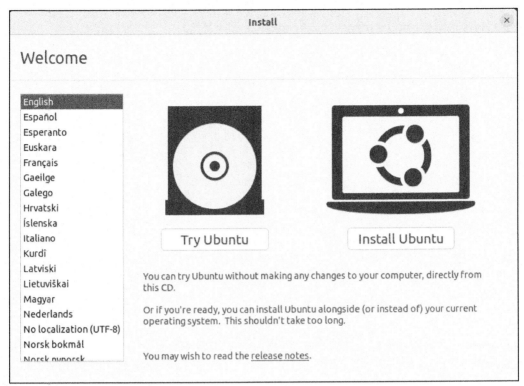

Figure 6.25

I will also need to select the appropriate language setting just like I did for Windows.

Next, I can choose what type of installation I want to perform. If I want the normal installation with all the apps and utilities I can choose *Normal installation*. If I just want the basics like a web browser then I can choose *Minimal installation*. If you really want to check out Linux and see what kind of apps come with the OS then you should go for the Normal installation.

Just like with Windows, Linux has regular updates such as fixes and security patches so if you want to have these updates downloaded during the installation you can check the box to do so.

Updates and other software

What apps would you like to install to start with?

⦿ Normal installation

    Web browser, utilities, office software, games, and media players.

○ Minimal installation

    Web browser and basic utilities.

Other options

☑ Download updates while installing Ubuntu

    This saves time after installation.

☐ Install third-party software for graphics and Wi-Fi hardware and additional media formats

    This software is subject to license terms included with its documentation. Some is proprietary.

Figure 6.26

The way Linux creates partitions on your hard drive for installing the OS differs from Windows so if this is a new PC with a blank hard disk then I would just go with the first option that says *Erase disk and install Ubuntu* under *Installation Type.* Then you will click the *Install Now* button.

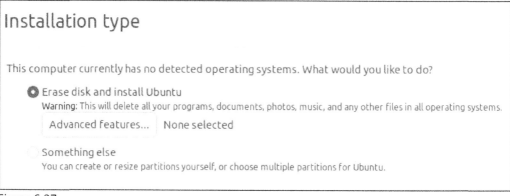

Figure 6.27

You will then get a warning saying the changes you have selected will be written to the disk and you can click on the *Continue* button to have them applied.

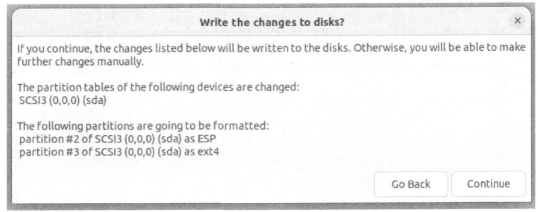

Figure 6.28

You will then be asked to choose your time zone before continuing.

Before using Linux for the first time you will need to create a username and password that will be used as your login account for the OS. Here you can also choose a name for the computer itself that will be seen on the network if you plan on doing any networking with this PC.

Who are you?

Your name: James

Your computer's name: UbuntuVM
The name it uses when it talks to other computers.

Pick a username: james

Choose a password: ●●●●●●●●● Good password

Confirm your password: ●●●●●●●●●

○ Log in automatically
● Require my password to log in

☐ Use Active Directory
You'll enter domain and other details in the next step.

Figure 6.29

Then it will go through the installation procedure after downloading the updates and install all the necessary files needed to run Ubuntu Linux on your computer.

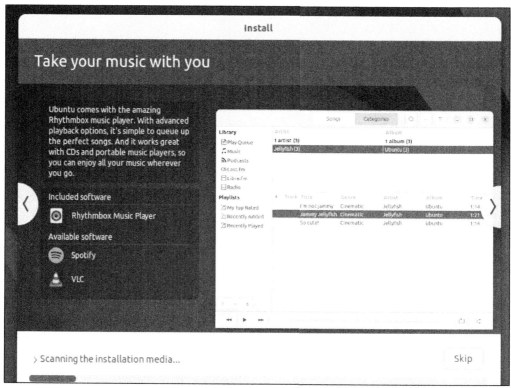

Figure 6.30

After a quick reboot, you will have your brand new Ubuntu Linux PC ready to go and you can then login and see how you like Linux.

Figure 6.31

What's Next?

Now that you have read through this book and are now an expert computer builder, you might be wondering what you should do next. Well, that depends on where you want to go. Are you happy with what you have learned, or do you want to further your knowledge or maybe get into a career in the IT (information technology) field?

If you do want to expand your knowledge, you should look at subject-specific books such as networking, storage, Windows, etc. Focus on one subject at a time, then apply what you have learned to the next subject.

There are many great video resources as well, such as Pluralsight or CBT Nuggets, which offer online subscriptions to training videos of every type imaginable. YouTube is also a great source for training videos if you know what to search for.

Once you have increased your knowledge a bit and want to get into the money-making side of computers, think about getting yourself some certifications on a couple of different subjects. For the basic computer repair area, you can go for the CompTIA A+ certification. For basic networking, you can take their Network+ exam, and for servers, they offer a Server+ exam. If you want a general type of certification, you can go for their IT Fundamentals certification. CompTIA used to have an exam for storage certification called Storage+, but that has since been retired. However, you can still take the SNIA Certified Storage Professional (SCSP) exam, which covers the same material.

If networking is more your thing, then think about some of the Cisco certifications. The most basic one you can take is the CCENT, and then you can consider moving your way up to the CCNA to prove you have what it takes to do the job. High level Cisco techs can make a lot of money, so if you enjoy working on switches and routers, this may be the path to take.

Of course, Microsoft offers a variety of certifications for various technologies, too. The most common certifications are for their server and domain platforms, such as the MCSE (Microsoft Certified Solutions Expert) and MCSA (Microsoft Certified Solutions Associate) certifications. They also offer lower level certifications such as the MTP (Microsoft Technology Associate) and MCP (Microsoft Certified Professional) certifications for subjects such as Windows 10.

What's Next?

Keep in mind that in the real world, experience matters more than certification. If you have a piece of paper saying you know something but you can't do it on the job, then it doesn't really help you out. Don't expect to start out at a high level, because it will take several years of practice to work your way up to the higher paying jobs.

If you are content in being a standalone computer geek that knows more than your friends, then just keep on reading up on the technologies you want to learn, and you will soon become your friends and family go-to computer person (which may or may not be something you want!).

Thanks for reading **Building Your Own Computer Made Easy**. You can also check out the other books in the Made Easy series for additional computer related information and training. You can get more information on my other books on my Computers Made Easy Book Series website.

https://www.madeeasybookseries.com/

You should also check out my computer tips website, as well as follow it on Facebook to find more information on all kinds of computer topics.

www.onlinecomputertips.com

https://www.facebook.com/OnlineComputerTips/

About the Author

James Bernstein has been working with various companies in the IT field for over 20 years, managing technologies such as SAN and NAS storage, VMware, backups, Windows Servers, Active Directory, DNS, DHCP, Networking, Microsoft Office, Exchange, and more.

He has obtained certifications from Microsoft, VMware, CompTIA, ShoreTel, and SNIA, and continues to strive to learn new technologies to further his knowledge on a variety of subjects.

He is also the founder of the website onlinecomputertips.com, which offers its readers valuable information on topics such as Windows, networking, hardware, software, and troubleshooting. James writes much of the content himself, and adds new content on a regular basis. The site was started in 2005 and is still going strong today.

Printed in Great Britain
by Amazon

36855565R00071